FLATLAND POINT

THE
DRAW & DRUM NAVIGATIONS

C. M. PETERSON

For John, whose love and joyful spirit
energize every wave!

*The strength of an impression,
however, proves nothing against
the fortuitous coincidence of all
these fishes.* C. G. Jung

TABLE OF CONTENTS

FLATLAND POINT

THE DRAW & DRUM NAVIGATIONS

C. M. PETERSON

"FLATLAND POINT is the locus where orthogonal waves pierce the sphere rather than wrap around it" ... with that, the cross fell off the wall onto my head. And from the vintage flowed the channel that Petroglyph Drummer, Mnemonic Plasma Surfer, and Synchronicity Cat speed down in reckless disregard for the No Wake Zone.

Tangible enough to be thrown over Brook's Bridge just at the moment of their crossing, flies this stash of spatial, temporal, and transcendent archetypal wave navigation. Had it been a mullet it might have flown right past but that is was a *bridle* of navigations, it stuck our friends to follow.

After bifurcating Specter Island, it's just three more river crossings to Flatland Point: "...like fringes emanating from some eternal honey-suckle, [synchronicity] returns... the result of a certain triturating of that once pure and supple lens...[t]he original self, *one fine day*, cut into little lunes so small as to impart no...slope...the transcendent granted return to timelessness as the next octave begins its reckoning in a luminous glow imbibing its tale."

THE DRUM NAVIGATION is a literature review of the popular use of drumming to experience that syncopated and resonant phenomenon opened by entraining our somatic and psychic grooves to plunge, surge, and spill on Flatland reef.

THE DRAW NAVIGATIONS are sketches we can use to guide our mandala of shadow friends to the flat-stanely-numen at the center of the reef. The

DRAW projective directives are proposed accompanied by a literature review of projective drawing methods used in psychology. A small data set is included with a first iteration qualitative analysis of drawings referencing Jung: "Drawing 3's sensuous content is nearly palatable: A man represented as hand held radio whose antenna emerges from the page in fastidious 3-D detail. The object's reality has been alienated; left to the mercy of the subjective shadow; it plays its part in an illusory myth amid flaring ambiguities and sordid possibilities."

This ideal reef material presents techniques, invites collaboration, and cites numerous scientific findings on drumming and drawing in the context of entrainment and projection.

PART 1: FLATLAND POINT

Therefore, in describing the living processes of the psyche, I deliberately and consciously give preference to a dramatic, mythological way of thinking and speaking, because this is not only more expressive but also more exact than an abstract scientific terminology, which is wont to toy with the notion that its theoretic formulations may one fine day be resolved into algebraic equations. C. G. Jung

CHAPTER 1: CERULEAN FRINGE

*One is as much
impressed by the
disharmony of things
as one is surprised by
their occasional
harmony.*   C. G. Jung

By Analogy...

A single line of swell moves in, wrapping around the point in a beautiful arc then plunges toward the center of the Flatland Point. Concentrically they follow, like a vast cerulean fringe gracing the point. At the center of this natural mandala sits the *image*, like a numen conducting the waves.

Indigenous watermen say that the waves converge on the point because their spirit is on a journey to the center locus. Countless ride the cerulean fringe but to see the central beckoning image you must go inside the Point.

• • •

A great many petroglyphic images of remarkably similar detail are found throughout the world; each accompanied with lore as diverse as the collective mindsets of the lands they are found. For example, one fellow you probably know is Kokopelli, the flautist who in some cultures opens portals to other realms; is a deity of fertility in other cultures; and an insect of trickster character in still another (Keyser & Klassen, 2001; Slifer, Nakai, & Mirabal, 2007). Now, plasma cosmologists, introducing a new collective mindset, attribute inspiration for these early images of Kokopelli to events caused by electrified plasma that filled the ancient terrestrial sky with fantastic, even terrifying spectacles resembling an entire cast of petroglyphical characters (Barkley, 2005; Hogan, 2007; Peratt, 2003; Talbot 2009). Archetypical petroglyph symbols of thunderbolts, scepters, chalices, human figures, and animals that appear in rock art all over the globe can be reproduced in plasma chambers and explained in terms of events occurring in the sky a few thousand years ago (Barkley; Hogan; Peratt; Talbot). The plasma discharge that forms the image of Kokopelli, a moment later forms the image seen in the Surfer petrography and later decays to a cross.

Figure 1: Kokopelli, Surfer and Drummer.

A stick figure flanked by two circles is another archetype symbol recorded in rocks, myths, and plasma experiments (Peratt, 2003). High energy instabilities of this image also look like a centipede, of perhaps even a surfer from a fish's perspective but we will call him Drummer here for obvious simplification. Talbott and Thornhill refer to him as a "squatter man" and find him in sacred designs throughout the world including the face of a Polynesian deity, and a Chinese longevity symbol. No matter what their source, it is clear that these ancient visitors, be they made of plasma or rock, have influenced culture and psyche. They are archetypes that entered our collective vision as if from another realm.

One could conjecture from a pragmatic point of view, that looking towards the sky at a large plasma discharge would look like a two dimensional slice of the archetype entering in and out of the terrestrials' view. Like Abbott's (1884) sphere entering Flatland, the circles that flank Drummer, when recreated in a three-dimensional plasma image, are spheres!

> *"Pardon me, my Lord," replied I; "but to my eye the appearance is as of an Irregular Figure whose inside is laid open to the view; in other words, methinks I see no Solid, but a Plane such as we infer in Flatland; only of an Irregularity which betokens some monstrous criminal, so that the very sight of it is painful to my eyes."* (Abbott; 1884; pg 69).

Drummer reminds us that where we believe in circles, there are actually spheres. Like the imagination of a child lying in the grass looking out at the stars, our vision is ever expanding. Where we see points there are galaxies. Imagine stars in infinite space; they would fill the fabric of the sky. Projections from infinite stars would fill-in all of the sky if time permitted their energy to travel the full journey. Their Lambert luminance casting shadows without fringes. *Seeing is believing*; when the energy from the sun illuminates the three-dimensional exterior volumetric-representation of an object; we believe in its existence. If by the Sun, *its* shadow is cast, *it* is a realism of objective fact, true.

In short, fringes are diffraction effects on the edges of a shadow. Speckle is the interference effect of light at the surface of an image plane. When the light is coherent, such as from a pet's laser pointer, these effects become more prominent. Scientists talk about "subjective speckle patterns" to describe the way the laser projection looks spotty to an observer and changes depending on how he looks at it; and "objective speckle patterns" which involves a phase induced by another's surface reflection.

Somewhere in the complexity of these seemly random speckles the *others* objective pattern correlates to the subjective pattern.

So in the light of the sun and extended constellations, my cat wags his tale and I believe it because I see it. Due here is a pause to tell you that the cat lying by my side, wagged his tale with an audible whack just at the moment of completing that sentence. The idea of it is so extraordinary; it seems impossible; statistically unlikely; even contrived to make the point. Yet a cat's wag is rarely so singular and voracious as to the cause pause to a writer, especially in the midst of conjuring a relevant metaphor! This fortuitous wag is an example of synchronicity. Synchronicity is a sort of acausal coincidence which we would otherwise discard as statistically unlikely in our typical daily, distracted, operating algorithms and perceptions. "Synchronicity therefore means the simultaneous occurrence of a certain psychic state with one or more external events which appear as meaningful parallels to the momentary subjective state—and, in certain cases, vice versa." (Jung, 1960). It seems that somewhere in the complexity of these seemly random moments of life the objective correlates to the subjective with strange vigor.

It seems the stuff of fringes and speckles. When we ride with the fringe we are synchronized, timeless.

CHAPTER 2: SPATIAL AND TEMPORIAL SHADOWS

How often have we not seen the truth condemned! C. G. Jung

By analogy to the Sun and stars, could we reasonably envision constellations of projection sources illuminating *that* which cast the shadows of our psyche? When the energy is coherent do we *see* the speckle, subjective to our perspective and objectified by others? As we expand our perception, antecedent algorithms, and operating principles, we embrace an extended harmony of perception (i.e. believe, truth) that includes the synchronicity of a cat's wag to a writers whim.

Without expanding our view beyond distraction-limited conventional mechanisms of causality, we are like sailors who have never seen the beach. Extending awareness to a degree which makes fringe synchronicity a tangible reality will be like expanding the sea out to the shore. If a sailor knew only how to sail offshore, how well could she manage a heavy point break? To her child born at sea, how absurd would be the *foam* that washes the Man O' War upon the sand?

A first-term optics experiment confirms a synchronistic effect. Green (2003) explains the classic Michelson interferometer experiment nicely for the non-scientific reader wherein a photon given two different possible paths always appears where the observer seeks it. Essentially, in the experiment, a single photon travels through a beam splitter which establishes two possible paths for the photon. The photon seems to split into twins, travel both paths, and rejoin with itself causing an interference effect where the paths merge. The photon, following its own repeatable criterion of behavior, appears to the consciousness of the observer, to be in two places at one time. With 100 percent statistical probability, the observer's consciousness observes the location of a photon exactly congruent to where it is sought.

The effect caused by interference of the photon and its shadow twin rejoining is as if the photon guessed what the observer would do. This experiment is analogous to Rhines experiment where a symbol on a card is determined as by a blind guess at a time previous to an observer drawing the card; to which Jung (1960) summarizes: "In these circumstances the time factor seems to have been eliminated by a psychic function or psychic condition which is also capable of abolishing the spatial factor" (p. 17).

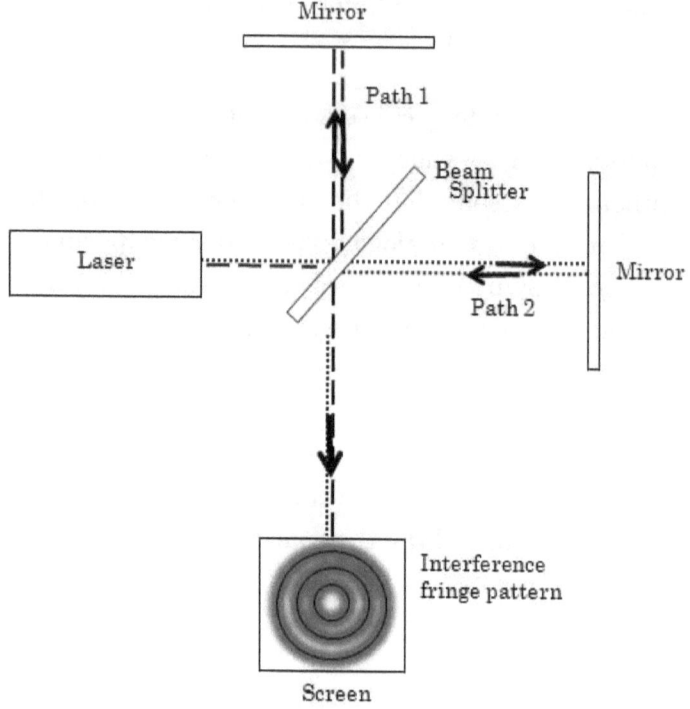

Figure 2: Michelson Interferometer.

A static concentric ring pattern is formed where the two paths of the Michelson Interferometer rejoin. The rings of the interference fringe pattern will expand outward or contract inward if slight changes are incurred along the paths (such as stage fog), creating a dynamic synchronized pattern now with a time dimension. The dynamic pattern seems to draw an aspirant observer in to infinite depths like one may experience in a trance. It is Mandala. This mandala is a not symbol; it is the objective and subject experience of the interference of energy at an image plane. Indeed it is a circular image with a concentric theme like those ritual circles associated with meditation, healing, and, prayer.

I am not a plane Figure, but a Solid. You call me a Circle; but in reality I am not a Circle, but an infinite number of Circles, of size varying from a Point to a Circle of thirteen inches in diameter, one placed on the top of the other. When I cut through your plane as I am now doing, I make in your plane a section which you, very rightly, call a Circle. For even a Sphere - which is my proper name in my own country - if he manifest himself at all to an inhabitant of Flatland - must needs manifest himself as a Circle. (Abbott; 1884)

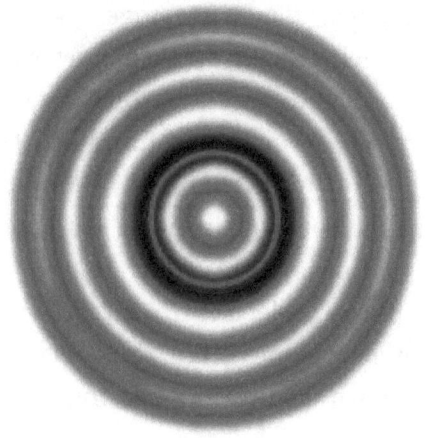

Figure 3: Interference fringe pattern. Infinite concentric circles collapse on the eternal locus of *where the fringes go*. This, my friend, is Flatland Point.

Our fringe figure collapses and expands as a sphere circumscribed by infinite circles, moving through the image plane however its diameter sustains. That its diameter does not diminish to zero or reach maximum (13 inches in Abbott's Sphere) indicates this *monstrous* creature passing through our image plane is not bound in merely 3 dimensions.

Moving the image plane about does not find the eternal loci either. Not even Upward; to follow the path through *where the fringes go*, we have to move into the center of the thing. We have to see inside.

Until the moment when I placed my mouth in his World, he had neither seen me, nor heard anything except confused sounds beating against - what I called his side, but what he called his inside or stomach; nor had he even now the least conception of the region from which I had come. Outside his World, or Line, all was a blank to him; nay, not even a blank, for a blank implies Space; say, rather, all was nonexistent. (Abbott, 1884).

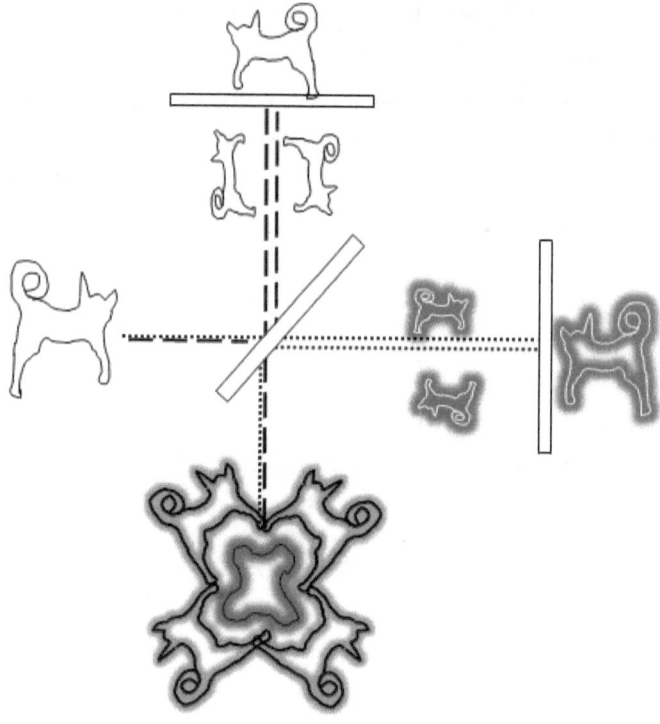

Figure 4: Idealistic Interferometer I: Cat and his Shadow stand-in to represent a photon following two paths to the psychic mandala.

Shadow is a term Jung used for the unconscious; it is one of three main Jungian archetypes along with and Anima and Animus. We could just as well have transposed the Anima or Animus into the Idealistic Interferometer as we did the Shadow.

Jung, writing about a dream:

The movement without friction shows that the clock is cosmic, even transcendental; at any rate it raises the question of a quality which leaves us in some doubt whether the psychic phenomenon expressing itself in the mandala is under the laws of space and time. And this points to something so entirely different from the empirical ego that the gap between them is difficult to bridge; i.e., the other centre of personality lies on a different plane from the ego since, unlike this, it has the quality of 'eternity' or relative timelessness." (Jung, 1944; p366).

Figure 5: Cat and Drummer in a Collective Idealistic Interferometer mandala.

Holography works on the principles of interferometry. In holography, laser reference fields interfere to create a volumetric representation of an object for conscious observation. We describe the conscious observation of the volumetric world by the way it is projected onto our senses from our point of view, our inertial frame. We also perceive projections from the inertial frame of our soul, psyche, and unconscious. The body-soul projection can be described in holographic terms where archetype reference fields interact.

Imagine a holographic display of a model aircraft in simulated flight. Just as the simulated aircraft's flight dynamics can be represented by Euler angles in the inertial frame of the aircraft, dynamics can also be represented from the frame of the holographic projector itself; in any case, the perspective is bound to its reference frame. The reference fields generating the interference patterns that create the holographic projection of the aircraft are projected from coherent laser sources embedded in the holographic projector devise.

The sources of the reference fields in the holographic realm create the perceivable world-constituting construct. As the reference field changes, so does the construct. The modality of the reference field is thus a preconditioned law within that holographic-world construct. However, whether driven by randomness or intention, modality of the sources varies with some quantum probability and gives rise to statistically anomalies. Some photons shift as contingent pre-cursors; some are latent; though most fall within a statistical Gaussian. Jung (1960) writes about this contingent of chance substrate on preconditioned law: "If we consider synchronicity or the archetypes as the contingent, then the latter takes on the specific aspect of modality that has the functionally significant world–constituting factors" (p. 99). This phase shifting of modalities may well give rise to our perception of time; the body or time-space modality being a harmonic of the soul's modality.

With more study, a classic wave-particle duality may be applied to the archetype-holographic analogy to elaborate on behavioral criterion. Consider the relationship of a photon to the complex interference patterns that cause the holographic construct; it is like the relationship of the point-of-view of an individual to the overall world-construct. Our point affects the whole and is yet a resultant instantaneous artifact of the intersection of reference fields passing through each other with dynamic modality. As such, our perception exists only as an instance of the summation of the exact state of all illuminating fields.

As with Abbott's (1884) King of Pointland, here we are, excited photon-like particles, imaged from a collection of archetypes, operating in a special instance of chance. So we create this consciousness to make sense of ourselves in a determinative, statistical, causal, and Cartesian, albeit latent, justification of our pointed perspective. The unconscious shadow twin stirring sweet rebellion:

> "Ah, the joy, ah, the joy of Thought!
> What can It not achieve by
> thinking! Its own Thought coming
> to Itself, suggestive of Its
> disparagement, thereby to enhance
> Its happiness! Sweet rebellion
> stirred up to result in triumph! Ah,
> the divine creative power of the All
> in One! Ah, the joy, the joy of
> Being!" (Abbott, 1884).

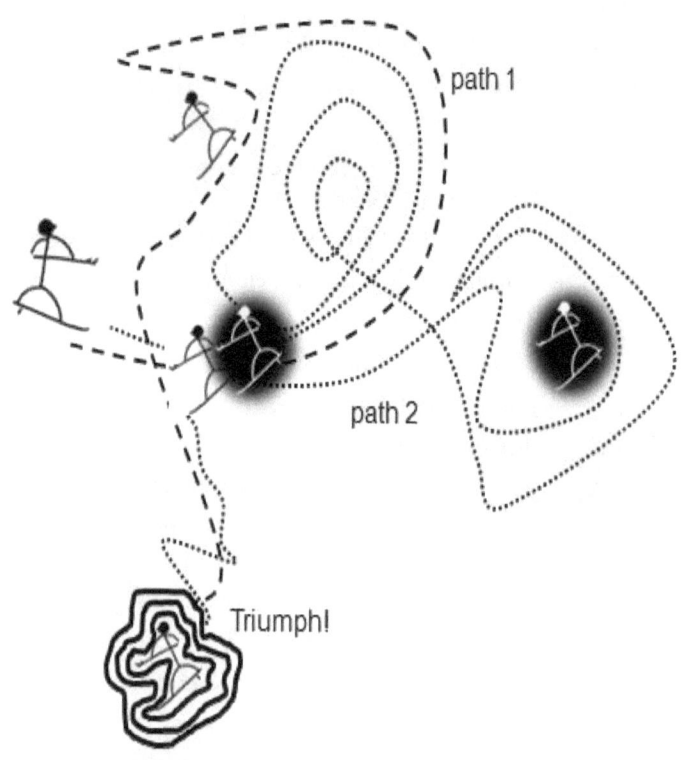

Figure 6: Idealistic Interferometer II: Surfer and Shadow stirred up in sweet rebellion.

Jung talks about the rebellion of the unconscious shadow:

> *The psychological rule says that when an inner situation is not made conscious, it happens outside as fate. That is to say, when the individual remains undivided and does not become conscious of his inner opposite, the world must perforce act out the conflict and be torn into opposing halves.*

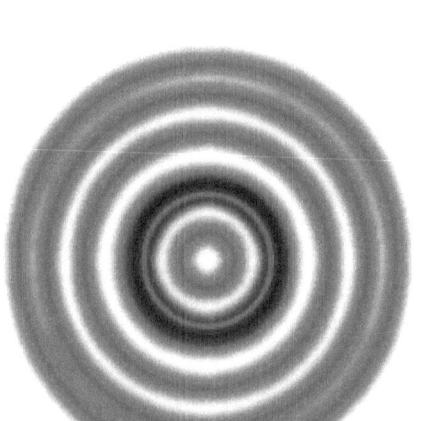

CHAPTER 3: FIFTH ELEMENT

Such a consciousness would see the becoming and passing away of things simultaneously with their momentary existence in the present, and not only that, it would also see what was before their becoming and will be after their passing hence." C. G. Jung

Throughout history, metaphors and mnemonics sustain a philosophical 4 or 5 element resonance to describe our nature. Empedocles used the elements Earth, Fire, Water, and Air as metaphors for the simple, eternal, and unalterable dynamic forces stirred up by Love and Strife that cause our existence. He also named these roots Zeus, Hera, Nestis, and Aideoneus who embody a perfect Sphere when the divine powers of Love and Strife are at rest. Aristotle's fifth element, Aether, is the numinous heavenly sphere stirring perpetual circular motion. The ancient Wu Xing cyclic movements are: Wood, Fire, Earth, Metal, and Water which correlate with the directions: East, South, Center, West, and North.

Hippocrates of Cos (~400 BC) limiting his concern to bodily functions named only 4 humors neglecting a divine 5th: black bile, yellow bile, phlegm, and blood. Accordingly, Theophrastus used Sanguine, Choleric, Melancholic and Phlegmatic to describe how people act when their humors are unbalanced. These four humors were then commonly associated with the ancient Air, Fire, Earth, and Water. The four continued their somatic journey leaving the numinous stirring of the 5th behind. The four, then are often represented in modern themes as: Artisan, Idealist, Guardian, Rational, and the Myers-Briggs' types of Sensation-Perceiving, Intuiting-Feeling, Sensing-Judging, and Intuiting-Thinking respectively. What happened to the transcendent 5th?

Mnemonic Plasma Surfer:

Since we used the Plasma element as a metaphor for archetypes earlier, let's use the meteorolgica elements here as symbolic mnemonics of the forces acting coherently within us to reintroduce the 5th in a tangible modern realm.

Consider our Surfer archetype: The essence of surfing integrates the waves' subjective and objective speckle: Water imbues through powerful currents. Air breathes the spirit of intuiting flow; Earth lines up with the terrestrial tribe. Fire ablates barrel and venom. Plasma soul centers. Latter Surfer meets Drummer at the campfire: Earth is grounded. Air is consumed with the ascending sparks. Water surges somatic echo waves. Fire is consecrated. Plasma radiates.

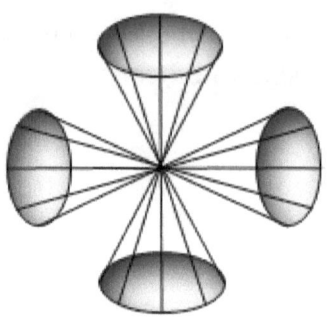

CHAPTER 4: ILLUMINATING ELEMENTS

Only a unified personality can experience life, not that personality which is split up into partial aspects, that bundle of odds and ends which also calls itself "man." C. G. Jung

Jung (1923) preserves the 5th; his four forces of personality, Objective and Subject; Rational and Irrational, are stirred by the Archetypes and the Collective Unconscious. However, later when Myers and Myers-Briggs sought to create an instrument based on Jung's theory (Myers & McCaulley, 1985; Varvel et al., 2004), they assigned four continuums with dichotomous end points derived from the functions and attitudes but left out Jung's emphasis on the recursive nature of the unconscious. Their model became one of the most popular personality inventories in the 20th century (Kennedy & Kennedy, 2004; McCaulley, 1990; Shank & Langmeyer, 1994) and as such has popular influence for a vast number of people.

In another modern adaptation, Hermmann (1996) combined Sperry's (1975) work on left and right brain thinking and Mclean's (1952) work on cerebral system and limbic system thinking to introduce his whole-brain model. When Sperry's left and right thinking types are placed along a continuum crossed by Mclean's cerebral and limbic continuum, the four quadrants of Hermmann's model emerge. Dawdy's (2006) Social Compass founded on positive psychology and emotional intelligence is another 4 quadrant example. It draws from research in the field of personality and behavior including Keirsey's temperament studies, and Marston's profile principles. Though the intersecting axes that define Hermann's cerebral, limbic, right, and left, differ from Dawdy's intersecting vectors, the models can be rotated such that each cardinal point of the compass falls within a whole-brain quadrant. A rotation of -135 degrees and swapping adjacent quadrants superimposes the models and lands them on top of the terminating nodes of Myers-Briggs' continuums (Meneely and Portillo;2005), aligned with the 4 bodily humors. Researchers comparing the Eysenck Personality Inventory and The Sixteen Personality Factor Questionnaire also report significant similarities.

These common models are understood to describe normal preferences and avoid confrontation with the transcendent. They are secular ways that people can talk about how they typically prefer to act and communicate in certain modes over others (Dawdy, 2006; DeRidder & Wilcox, 1999). Even though we have our preferred style we actually integrate elements of each, be they compass headings, humors, or any other mnemonic. The mnemonic plasma surfer helped us illustrate this point.

Consciously connecting with the forces within us and our friends expands our awareness of human diversity. Expanded awareness facilitates adaptive environments (Karagiannidis & Sampson, 2002). Thus, it is not surprising that personality awareness is becoming widely sought in organizational arenas. Following are general definitions from common adaptations of the quadratic dichotomies. More discussion on Jung's psychological types will be presented latter in the qualitative discussion of the DRAW data.

Introversion–Extraversion (Objective-Subjective) Dichotomy:

Jung (1923) described the extroverted attitude as objective and the introverted as subjective. Sometimes looking at the limits of a thing helps us define it: "Introverted thinking carried to extremes arrives at the evidence of its own subjective existence, and extroverted thinking at the evidence of its complete identity with the objective fact." (Jung, p. 239). In adaptations, the introversion-extraversion dichotomy is generally defined as how an individual focuses his or her mental energies (Rosswurm, Pierson, & Woodward, 2007). *Introvert* refers to an individual who focuses his or her mental energy on constructs related to the inner world (Offir, Bezalel, & Barth, 2007). *Extravert* refers to an individual who focuses mental energy on external objects or social constructs (Francis, Craig, & Robbins, 2007). "We could say that introverted sensation transmits an image which does not so much reproduce the object as spread over it the patina of age-old subjective experience and the shimmer of events still unborn. The bare sense impression develops in depth, reaching into the past and future, while extraverted sensation seizes on the momentary existence of things open to the light of day. (Jung, p 254.)

Judging–Perceiving (Rational-Irrational) Dichotomy

The judging-perceiving dichotomy generally refers to the dichotomous preference of how a person interprets information and reacts to incoming stimuli (Sak, 2004). An analogy can be drawn to the rout teaching of elementary school vs. the holism of academia. Judging types are termed *rational* because they are grounded on the functions of rational judgment; perceiving types are termed *irrational* because their actions are not based on rational judgment but the sheer intensity of perception (Jung, 1923). Thus, *Judging* refers to a person's preference toward using his or her ration preference, thinking or feeling. *Perceiving* is an individual's preference toward using the irrational preferences, intuiting or sensation (Ellis, 2003). Jung describing the irrational: "Their perception is directed simply and solely to events as they happen, no selection being made by judgment. In this respect they have a decided advantage over the two judging types".

Sensation–Intuition Dichotomy (Irrational)

The sensation-intuition dichotomy refers to how a person prefers to perceive incoming information (Craig et al., 2006). *Sensation* type personalities prefer to rely on fact and observation that can be collected by the five senses (Goby, 2006). *Intuiting* personality types prefer to think unbound by senses and relate information to abstract thinking and conceptualizations (Boyd & Brown, 2005). The sensation function sensually perceives objects while the intuitive function reads into what is seen in the object. Discussing conscious extroverted intuition, Jung (1923) clarifies: "Just as sensation when it is the dominant function, is not a mere reactive process of no further significance for the object, so intuition is not mere perception, or vision , but an active, creative process that puts into the object just as much as it takes out." (p221). Jung characterized the extraverted sensation type as having an extraordinarily developed sense of realism. Differentiating between the introverted sensing and intuiting, Jung explains: "Just as the world of appearances can never become a moral problem for the man who merely senses it, the world of inner images is never a moral problem for the intuitive. For both of them it is an aesthetic problem, a matter of perception, a sensation." (p. 260).

Thinking–Feeling Dichotomy (Rational)

The thinking-feeling dichotomy refers to the dichotomous preference of how a person makes decisions and is considered a judgment preference (Ross, Francis, & Craig, 2005). *Thinking* personality types prefer to reason things impersonally and often rely on logic and fact to make decisions (Wheeler, Hunton, & Bryant, 2004). *Feeling* personality types make decisions based on other people's feelings, moral standards, and social desirability (Howell, 2004). For the feeling type, ideas are felt and actions are guided by feelings. For the thinking type, ideas are thought and actions are determined by thinking. Both of these types live their life subordinated to rational judgment (Jung, 1923).

Principle and Auxiliary Functions

People do not align purely with a single function; a secondary function is always paired with the primary function such that a primary rational function, thinking or feeling, is paired with a secondary irrational function, sensing or intuiting. If the primary function is the irrational, then the auxiliary function is rational and the other way around (Jung, 1923). The secondary function is complimentary; it cannot be a function that is in opposition to the primary. Jung explains: "Hence the auxiliary function is possible and useful only in so far as it serves the dominant function without making any claim to the autonomy of its own principle." (p. 268). Jung explains that correlative unconscious rational and irrational attitudes balance each function as well. For example, the correlative of conscious, thinking may be an unconscious, intuitive-feeling attitude.

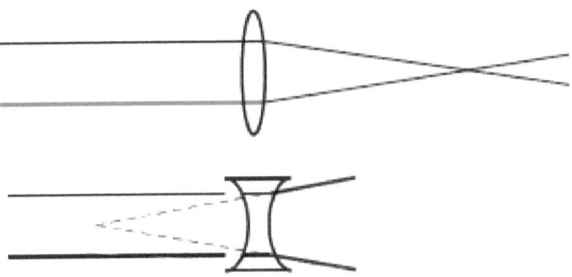

CHAPTER 5: A FUNDAMENTAL OPTICS MODEL OF SELF

The "squaring of the circle" is one of the many archetypal motifs which form the basic patterns of our dreams and fantasies. But it is distinguished by the fact that it is one of the most important of them from the functional point of view. Indeed, it could even be called the archetype of wholeness. C. G. Jung

When Hippocrates' 4-quadrant flat human is turned on his side, his personality is hidden inside the plane of the 4 quadrants, indistinguishable from others. Another human then turned to her side orthogonal to the first would then appear just a line. We may, as the Chromatistes (Abbott, 1884) then turn to adornment to reveal a contrived identity, whether true or deceitful. Instead, if we were to expand the dimensionality of our perception we could see inside both the male and female planes. However if we limit the expansion to only one direction (as with time) we would only have a clear view of one orientation of our orthogonal friends. Moving off axis for a moment (a slight mode shift in the reference field) would give us an, albeit skewed, glimpse of further fringe archetypes.

Perhaps consult with Hippocrates of Chios, who endeavoring to achieve quadrature of a circle (squaring the circle) introduced the cube root, would have expanded his namesake's representation of the humors. In his work, Hippocrates of Chios devised "lunes" which are segments drawn to calculate the area of a circle—an approach left incomplete due to the transcendental nature of pi (π). Transcendental pi (π) lumes as the beacon for inquiry beyond the sphere and tells us that representation of the archetypes in cubic realm will not be complete. For that quest we will have to journey to Flatland Point.

But let's not delay for the "one fine day" (Jung, 1959, p. 151) when the living character is carved up into little pieces and glued together with equations. Before we open Bohm (1951), let's take out our Jenkins and White (1976) and consider a transcendent fundamental optics model.

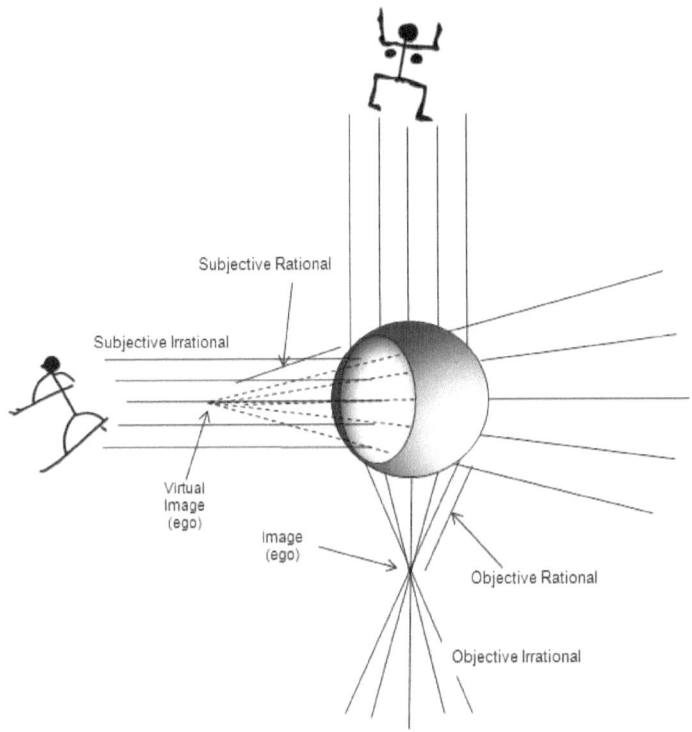

Figure 7. Transcendent Fundamental Optics Model using the analogy of archetypal wave fronts imaged through a 3 dimensional lens.

At the center of the Transcendent Fundamental Optics Model (Figure 7) is a lens having convergent (+) optical power along one axis and divergent (-) optical power along another (not necessarily orthogonal). It is used here to represent a transcendent function. Jung (1976; original work 1916) defines the transcendent function as a psychological function comparable to a mathematical function (in this case an optical function) which is a function of real and imaginary numbers and says that the psychological transcendent arises from "the union of conscious and unconscious contents" (p 273). Only two axes of the lens are shown here for simplicity of the 2 dimensional page front and discussion; however, one could consider spatial, temporal, chromatic, density, resonant, and energy constituent complexities of the model as it is discussed.

Drummer and the Surfer are standing in as archetypes, numina, or anything else you would like to consider imaged through this transcendent model. A wave front imaged from far away (distance approaching infinity) is represented by parallel lines. As the infinitely distant archetypal image intersects the lens along the convergent axis, the energy is focused into an image in objective space. As the image intersects the lens along the divergent axis, energy fans out as if emanating from a focal point before the lens; the virtual image thus created in subjective space. Likewise, remember that a lens' power is never turned-off (except in the absence of light) and works in both directions; therefore, the divergent axis collimates the subjective energy while the convergent axis collimates the objective energy.

The rational functions of judging (i.e. thinking and feeling), converge between the transcendent function (lens/self) and the image. The irrational functions of perception (i.e. sensing and intuiting), are collimated by the lens (self) in a pure sense to the eye of the archetype. Likewise energy from the infinitely distance archetype is transformed by the lens (self), imaged through the ego, and dispersed. Thus the dispersed energy of the archetype can then be collected, imaged through a different ego, and collimated by that ego's self for the transmission to another archetype. That archetype is assumed to have an inertial frame in a psychic sense, created from the intersecting arrival of collimated reference fields (holographic). Should the self lack the power or purity (i.e. if aberrations are incurred) then the energy will be thus affected and, not completely collimated, fall short of carrying its full energy in that single direction of infinite travel. The energy will then eventually diverge (forming unconscious virtual images in objective space), possibly converging along its way (forming the unconscious real images in subjective space), skewing the arriving reference field and thus intrinsically skewing the collective archetype.

Primary and Auxiliary Functions in the Model

Primary and auxiliary functions work together in rational-irrational pairs. In the model, the auxiliary function locates the focal point to image the ego and the primary function collimates the image. Thus for a primary objective irrational (perceiving) type, the auxiliary rational (judging) function determines where the object lies to be perceived. For a primary objective rational (judging) type, the auxiliary irrational (perceiving) function determines where the object lies to be judged. For a primary subjective irrational (perceiving) intuiting type, the auxiliary rational (judging) function determines the origin of divergent cone, range, or extent to be perceived. For a primary subjective rational (judging) type, the auxiliary irrational (perceiving) function constructs the objects for judgment in the subjective space.

How far the image (ego) extends from the lens (self) can be thought of as a matter of relative aperture or f-number. We can talk about depth of field. When we have a high f-number (i.e. long depth of field) the sharpness of the image is constrained by diffraction whereas a low f-number lens is limited by aberrations. It is not surprising then that a person may say he feels small, focused, and to the point when thinking and sees the big picture when intuiting; a long range vision looks fuzzy; and a close inspection reveals ones true color. A low f-number is associated with the rational functions and a high f-number is associated with the irrational functions. Differentiation within the rational (thinking, feeling) and irrational (sensing, intuiting) functions may be attributed to aberrations and diffraction effects respectively.

As you look at the model, you see the Objective Rational energy converging to a real image in objective space; this ego says: 'I perceive in order to objectively judge; perceiving is secondary'. Objective Irrational energy converges on a real image in object space; this ego says: 'I judge to objectively validate perception; judging is secondary.' Subjective Rational energy converges to a virtual image in subjective space; this ego says: 'I perceive in order to subjectively judge; perceiving is secondary'. And in the model, the pure Subjective Irrational does not converge to an image but rather creates a standing wave with the archetype; the ego formed at nodes of the standing wave says: 'I judge to subjectively validate perception; judging is secondary'.

Our lens (self) is subject to diffraction and aberrations. That which we are tuned to will focus most clearly. We hear folks say things like: she is really tuned in to her feelings; trying to get on your wavelength; or that really resonates with me. We can make sense of the images that we are tuned to; others are distorted, wrong, or obscured. We adjust our perceptions and judgments by tuning in.

If the self lens did not cause any transformation, in essence was not present, then the self would have no effect on the *energy* fields in which it occurs (here, the word energy is used to simplify the discussion). If the self lens was perfectly collimating in all directions for all functions then it would be a pure conduit of energy between the infinite archetypes. With no transcendence, there is no slope to measure divergence or convergence and thus no change over time; time is eliminated; ego is eliminated.

Tertiary Repression of Synchronicity

Assume for a moment that our lens begins as pure and supple, perfectly collimating without ego. Then as we are emerge in time, thus giving a meaning to the word *beginning*, our lens shapes forming ego. Time, now in the picture as an offset from the original equilibrium state of pure collimation, modulates the lens about the equilibrium state forming multiple egos.

That our ego will be dominated by our primary and secondary objective- subjective, rational-irrational pair (notice we are still keeping within powers of 2) necessitates a balancing pull from our tertiary and quaternary pair. Thus, for example, the aims of an original intuiting thinker will be tempered with feeling and sensing. The tertiary acting as balancing force, an unconscious opponent having the quality of opposite gender (Jung, 1923) steps in strongest to quall the mission of the primary which, in the case of an irrational primary is toward collimation, i.e. no slope, the end of time, return to synchronicity. For the primary intuiting, the tertiary repressing dependence of synchronicity, masquerades as feeling as if to defend from being let down or duped when he can no longer achieve the supple riches of infancy, i.e. the infinitely collimated, synchronous, resonance with the archetype.

Return to Synchronicity

If it happens that are conceived by nectar of synchronicity; as neonates we thrive by its sweet smell; as infants we know beauty by it; as children we pluck its strings resonating stigma (anima) and anthers (animus) nodes; as teens we adorn ourselves with its tricks; as distracted adults we all but vanquish it; and in maturity, like fringes emanating from some eternal honey-suckle, it returns; then can we suggest that this is the result of a certain triturating of that once pure and supple lens? The original self, *one fine day*, cut into little lunes so small as to impart no refraction, no image, no slope. The energy transversing the transcendent granted return to timelessness as the next octave begins it reckoning in a luminous glow imbibing its tale along the eternal journey to Flatland Point.

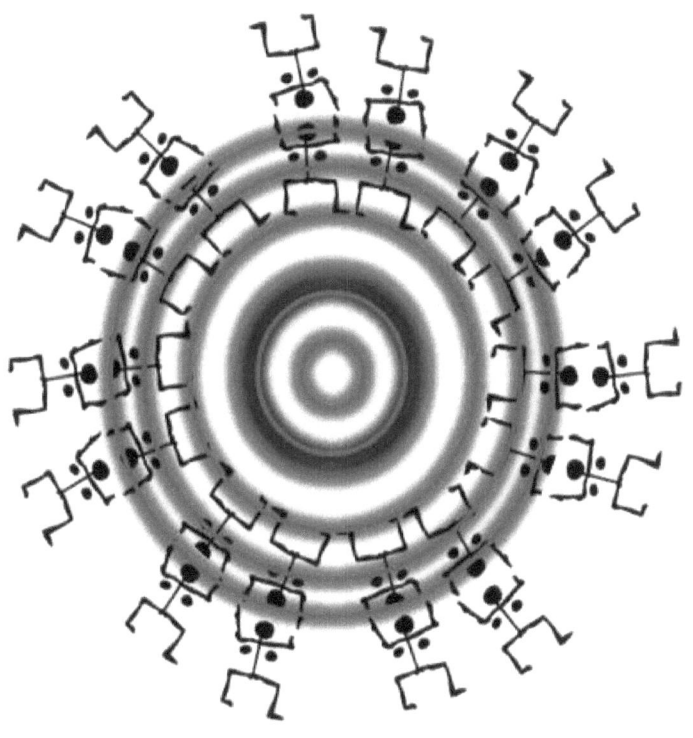

PART 2: DRUM

Whatever you do you have to like it; I don't know if that's a problem with logic. James Dean

CHAPTER 6: TEMPORAL AND MELODIC ARCHETYPES

That is the great secret of art, and of its effect upon us. The creative process, so far as we are able to follow it at all, consists in the unconscious activation of an archetypal image, and in elaborating and shaping this image into the finished work. By giving it shape, the artist translates it into the language of the present, and so makes it possible for us to find our way back to the deepest springs of life. C. G. Jung.

When the head of the drum is struck it acts like a lens projecting sound. As the surface of the lens modulates so does the focus of energy; sound images move in and out of focal planes modulating between rational and irrational; objective and subjective. Easily we feel the influence of adjacent drums' energy on our own. The rhythm becomes enjoyable, entrained, and collective. Egos dance; selves resonate.

Along with petroglyphs, ancient cultural groups told their stories with music. Sure songs help us to remember words and thus pass on information throughout the ages; but it is the emotional effect of the music that passes and preserves the salient message. A picture is no story without a resonance to arouse and reinforce emotions. Readers sharing my intrigue of synesthesia may intuitively perceive a sustained rhythm of the petroglyphs.

Drumming is emerging as a viable technique for creating synergy in diverse modern groups. The phenomenon seems new, as if a certain modern day critical mass of folks we were just opening an email sent from ancient groups over the *synchroneity-internet*. Through drawing and drumming ancient groups created the virtual image of their world and blind-copied it to us in rhythmic and visual forms. Today, one reaches for a pen, whiteboard marker, teleconference, or computer graphics program to explain a concept to a colleague. When knowledge sharing is ineffective, and tolerance decreased, folks search for a common ground. The ground from which we can reference synergistic potential has temporal and spatial resonance.

Sculpting and projecting music influences psychic states. Emotional expression in music has been discussed among the world's greatest philosophers since the earliest periods of history. Empirical study of the expressive qualities of music is of vast importance to social and cultural psychology (Strecker, 2001). People respond differently to music depending on personality and emotional state (Krumhansl, 2002).

We like to listen to music because of the feeling the music elicits; often that feeling or emotional response is not entirely positive. Listening to a particular style of music may induce negative emotional responses especially in people with social or mental disorders (Krumhansl). On average, by the time we reach high school, we have spent the same amount of time being influenced by musicians as we have by our classmates and teachers (Schwartz) perhaps far more.

Music is a complex temporal structure. We can discuss the subjective nature of music as an art form, its psychological influences, and social relevance. Music compositions can be comprised of a very simple single-line melody or a staggeringly complex symphony of melodies, counter melodies, and wide harmonic variations; each eliciting great emotional variance (Bigland, Viellard, Madurell, Marozeau, & Dacquet, 2005). We perceive music in a very personal way. Two listeners will rarely relate the same emotional experience from the same composition (Jeong & Joung, 1998).

The number of musical structures that produce emotional response is stunning. A note is a specific unit of rhythm. The basic unit of rhythm is the quarter note, which is equal to one beat. There are many different kinds of notes each corresponding to a different unit of rhythm and they can be linked to form continuous sounds or they may signify rests, which are units of rhythm that are silent. When pitches are assigned to notes, they form the audible sequence called the melody (Demany & Semal, 2002). Melody consists of a string of notes with pitches applied to each of the notes. Pitch is the frequency at which an audio wave resonates. Pitches are arranged in intervals according to musical archetypes; in western music pitches are arranged such that there are 12 evenly spaced pitches per octave. An octave is the interval of two pitches with the second pitch having twice the frequency of the first; i.e. squaring the 12th root. The first pitch would sound lower than the last because the frequency is slower (Demany & Semal, 2002). Pitches arranged in a series are called a mode.

There are many different mode variations; however, most modes are defined as major, minor, or atonal (Gagnon & Peretz, 2003). Musicians usually communicate these ideas in a very subjective manner, often referring to the way a musical structure sounds by analogy and metaphor.

Melody

The sounds of melodies are often referred to by metaphors that describe a certain feeling or emotion (Woody, 2002). Understanding how the mind perceives melody is clearly important to understanding how humans perceive and respond to musical stimulus. Expressions such as bouncy, smooth, flowing and liquid are often applied to describe the sound of the melody. Woody noted that instructors use these analogies to teach musicians how to develop proper melodic phrasing and to communicate the intended emotional qualities.

In their study concerning the interactive effects of various music stimuli Webster and Weir found tonality of melody played the most significant role in altering the listeners' emotional responses to selected test compositions. Lise Gagnon and Isabelle Peretz (2003) found that the tonality of the melody directly affected emotions; their research participants confirmed that minor modes felt sad, and major modes were happy. Lindstrom (2003) also asserted that minor melodies produce angry emotional responses and that major melodies are often perceived as sounding tender.

Rhythm

Rhythm is the fundamental basis of all music. Sound devoid of rhythm is not music (Demany & Semal, 2002). Musically, rhythm provides the metric standard to arrange pitches within melodies and for their harmonization to make sense. Iwao Yoshino and Jun-ichi Abe (2004) defined metrical organization as the process of arranging pitches in a coherent metrical structure. While Yoshino and Abe's research focused primarily on melody, their research made it clear that the perception of melody would be nearly impossible without some form of metric or rhythmic standard. There are many different aspects of rhythm that deal with differing levels of temporal organization.

Rhythm in its most basic form acts as a time keeper and is called tempo. The tempo of a composition is measured by the number of beats per time (Webster & Weir, 2005). In a study concerning how different musical stimuli react with each other, tempo was found to cause a wide range of modification to the listener's perception of emotion (Juslin & Laukka, 2004). Juslin and Laukka found that high tempos are associated with happiness when paired with major melodic tonality and anger when paired with minor or atonal melodic tonality. They also theorized that higher tempos might not only elicit modified emotional responses, but might also increase emotional sensitivity or arousal and illicit high energy responses from listeners.

A higher tempo also seems to require a higher level of cognitive activity to comprehend, thus it requires more concentration and absorbs more of the listeners attention. This leads the listener not only to experience an emotion, but also to experience that emotion with more intensity as the rhythm brings the whole of the listener's cognitive functions to focus on the music (Blood, Zatorre, Bermudez, & Evans, 2005). High tempos might also lead the listener to perceive the music very negatively (Crawley, Acker-Mills, Pastore, & Weil, 2002). This is because the complex auditory scenes of music can be very difficult for the brain to organize if the tempo is too high causing the music to be perceived as unpleasant (Crawley et al.).

Slow tempo is theorized to imply sadness (Peretz & Zatorre, 2005). However, slow tempos seem to exhibit the same attributes of higher tempos in that slow tempos appear to simply modify the melodic structure. A slow tempo paired with a minor melody is perceived as sad while a slow tempo with a major melody may be perceived to be tender or caring (Juslin & Laukka, 2004).

Changing tempo also causes emotional responses. One example is when a slow tempo is suddenly shifted to a tempo twice the original speed eliciting an emotional reaction heightened by the reflected melodic structure. This is a dynamic quality of rhythm that is often employed alongside changes in volume to startle listeners and create tension and resolution (Ravaja & Kallinen, 2004).

Tempo of an irregular nature is also useful in a composition. Irregular rhythms are sometimes used to create compositions that seem as though they have an incomplete or chaotic quality. Masterfully, these irregular patterns are then arranged such that common melodies immerge and can be recognized within the irregular rhythmic context. Melodies created using these irregular patterns create a sense of tension and release as the mind integrates the convergences of the tempo and melody (Demany & Semal, 2002). Tension and repose are directly responsible for the emotional responses of listeners and are often used to focus emotional stimulus in a performance setting (Canaza, De Poli, Roda, & Vidolin, 2003).

Composition

When integrated with dexterity, musical sub-structures develop tension, repose, resolution, and expectations (Tillman & Bigand, 2004). Rhythm, melody, tone, and pitch, work cohesively to produce the nodes of tension, repose, and resolution (Krumhansl, 2002). Changing dynamics elicits expectation. For example, the composer may cleverly use dynamic ambiguity in the arrangement of scenes to elevate the listeners' expectation for the composition to resolve itself and become consolidated and direct. If a composition succeeds in validating the expectation of the listener by elevating and resolving the tension, it will have a strong emotional effect (Krumhansl, 2002).

A composer may also use polyphony and high order chord harmonization to allow the listener to beautifully integrate several separate audio scenes effortlessly or conversely cause divergence, straining the listeners' attention. This divergence creates emotional tension (Foret, Bigand, & McAdams, 2000). Similarly, the composer may use divergent and convergent melody and countermelody to create and relieve tension. An effective composer has the ability to layer scenes. When those scenes are skillfully composed, such that the human mind can effortlessly integrate them, a very pleasing effect is created (Foret et al). We flow with the energy when it is synchronized with our subjective fringe.

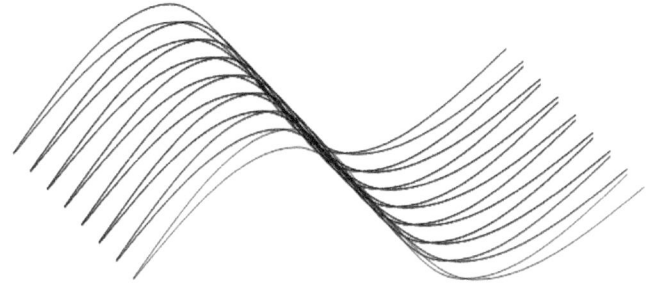

CHAPTER 7: RESONANTING SYNERGY

So it is not surprising that when an archetypal situation occurs we suddenly feel an extraordinary sense of release, as though transported, or caught up by an overwhelming power. At such moments we are no longer individuals, but the race; the voice of all mankind resounds in us. C. G. Jung

The basic nature of our relationship to the world is rhythm. In nature it is binding glue. Musically it is the perception of order. For people it is the way to harmony. Rhythm synchronizes the mind, body, and heart, creating shared moments of cohesion and joy (Hull, 1998; Kalani, 2004; Stevens, 2003).

Drumming Rhythm Circles

More and more drumming is recognized as an important and informative domain to study a variety of aspects of cognition and culture (Honing, 2006). Drumming is an artistic and cultural process. Artistic and cultural processes nourish people's capacity to listen, empathize, communicate, and trust (Yalen & Cohen, 2007). It is not surprising, then that people in all sorts of arenas enjoy drumming as a fun, nonthreatening way to experience synergy, harmony, and growth. Yalen and Cohen note that such exercises can transform relationships divided by conflict into relationships of interdependence and trust. Drumming together provides an arena for rehumanizing; empathizing; as well as imaging and sustaining positive social change.

Most cultures have drummed for rituals, celebrations, and ceremonies; they tap into a "primal need to share and support one another through one of the simplest and most beautiful ways to connect without words; music" (Stevens, 2003; p. 11). Winkelman (2003) stated that drumming induces relaxation; increases self-awareness, insight, and psychological integration; provides a secular approach to applying spiritual perspectives to psychological and emotional dynamics; and fills social needs for connectedness with other and interpersonal support.

Drumming can be a shared recreational experience of play rather than performing. This type of play transcends the boundaries of language and culture. Drumming engages people in the universal qualities of sharing, cooperation and focusing on a common goal (Kalani, 2004). People get together to drum for all sorts of reasons. To name just a few: there are community drum circles which create opportunities for socializing or spiritual growth; educational drum activities; health and wellness drumming groups; and facilitated teambuilding drum activities in corporate settings.

Universal Rhythm

All things in nature have rhythm. From the largest universal systems to the smallest sub-atomic mazes, all things exist as positive and negative energy states oscillating in rhythmic synergy (Schrodinger, 1982). Whether described as strings, particles, or waves propagating in a time and space continuum, modern physics recognizes the universal existence of rhythm (Hawking & Penrose, 1996). The rhythm of things seeks a sympathetic synergy (Letiche, & Hagemeijer, 2004). Dutch scientist, Christiaan Huygen wrote about rhythmic synergy in a letter to his father:

> ...*I have noted an impressive effect which no one has yet been able to explain. This is that two clocks, hanging side by side and separated by one or two feet, keep between them a consonance so exact that the two pendula always strike together, never varying.* (Huygens in Nijhoff, 1893)

Physicists have come to call this coupling together of frequencies in physical systems, *mode-locking* or *entrainment* (Spoor & Swift, 2000). Entrainment is the tendency for things, oscillating in nature, to phase-lock, i.e. vibrate in harmony; it is the synchronization of rhythmic cycles (Spoor & Swift). The principle of entrainment is observed universally; observations throughout physics, chemistry, biology, psychology, and sociology show that systems phase-lock oscillations, i.e. synchronize, to transfer energy between them (Hyson, 2003).

Rhythmic Entrainment

Entrainment forms the basis for social coordination (Schmidt & O'Brien in Newell & Molenaar, 1998). Physiological, psychological and interpersonal human behavior is temporal, rhythmical, cyclical and oscillatory in character; endogenous rhythms are inherent in all of the life process (Clayton, Sager & Will, 2004; McGrath & Kelly, 1986). As early as the 1930s, American anthropologist, Chapple, found that normal social interactions of humans are rhythmically organized; biological rhythmic processes range from ultradian, very fast (eg. brain waves and muscle fibre firings) to infradian longer periods (eg. menstrual cycles and migration pattern; Chapple, 1970).

A classic example of how humans rhythmically entrain to each other is the interpersonal coordination dynamics of people walking together, their strides matching in unison (Shin'ya et al. 2005). Another example is that when individual pulsing heart muscle cells are brought close together, they beat in synchrony (Jalife, 1984).

To a musician rhythmic entrainment, the sympathetic naturalism of interrelatedness, describes the well-known phenomenon of syncopation often referred to as *groove* (Whiteley, 1997). The groove entrained between the musical performers is extended into somatic properties such as dance (Hawkins in Whiteley, 1997). Musicians and non-musicians synchronize to drum beating with somatic movements of considerable interindividual consistency reflecting psychological dimensions independent of musical genre and style (Madison, 2006). The groove rides the entrainment fringe to converge on our somatic and shadow experience resonating between rebellion and triumph!

A compelling evolutionary view of biomusicology contextualizes socio-emotional confluence signaling in musical rhythmic behavior (Graham, 2006). Confluence signaling suggests the necessity of rhythmic entrainment to biomusical erotic somatic interaction (Whiteley, 1997). McNeil (1995) theorized that human's ability to dance together has facilitated our evolutionary speed. Through entrainment flows the nectar of synchronicity.

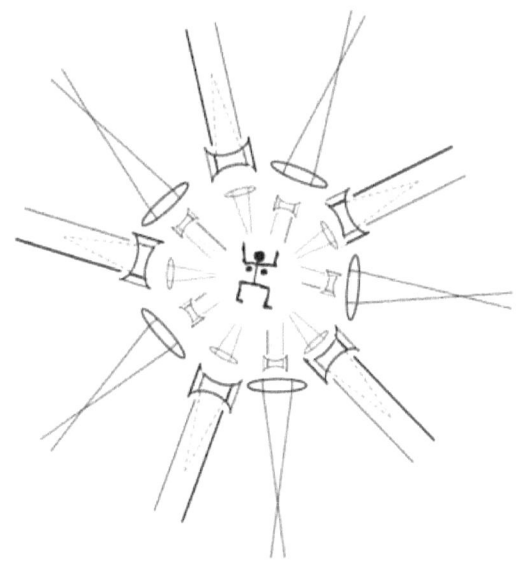

CHAPTER 8: CULTURAL SYNERGY

The normal man can follow the general trend without injury to himself; but the man who takes to the back streets and alleys because he cannot endure the broad highway will be the first to discover the psychic elements that are waiting to play their part in the life of the collective . C. G. Jung

Rhythmic entrainment is one of the fundamental processes of connection between individuals and the cultural world around them (Clayton, Sager, & Will, 2004). Interaction synchrony in verbal and non verbal communication across cultures is a temporal, interactive experience: the perceived rhythms set up expectations in the listener (decoder) based on the current context and schemata learned in cultural experiences (Clayton, Sager, & Will, 2004).

The term social entrainment is used to describe a social system as a set of coupled or entrained social and cultural interactions between human individuals requiring negotiated temporal order and synchronization of individual's activity cycles (McGrath & Kelly, 1986). Ethnomusicologists analyze this rhythmic synchronization in terms of social condition and implications (Clayton, Sager & Will, 2004). The socio-emotional confluence of rhythmic entrainment is tempered by social and cultural constructs (Iyer, 2003).

When people drum a rhythm for an extended period of time, their brain waves synchronize entrained to the rhythm, creating unity and harmony (Redmond 1997). Drumming sustained on the order of 15 minutes can be correlated with changes in brainwave frequency and subjective experience (Maxfield, 2006). Experiential synchrony extends temporal entrainment; the stronger the initial entrainment, the better coupling into new zeitgeber (Ancona & Chong, 1992).

Rhythmic entrainment is a prime mover in social relations; rhythm links people by providing a common cultural framework that facilitates group activities and identification, coordinating energies and resources in work and social discourse, exchange of information and expressive acts (Lomax, 1982). Rhythmic entrainment creates social order and function (Collier & Burch, 1998). Entrainment at the social level spans the natural limits of time; driving a range of temporal resonance from very fast sensory impulses to slow changes such as fashion and art (Collier & Burch). Collier and Burch suggest that even the fall of the Berlin Wall is attributable to rhythmic social entrainment.

A group's experience of time is created and sustained through task related communication (Ballard & Seibold, 2003). Task related communication increases cohesiveness and opens minds. Mickey Hart's (1991) Testimony before the U.S. Senate Committee on Aging addressed the importance of sharing rhythm; he reminded the committee that people love to play with rhythm and explained how a collective voice realized through entrainment evokes a group consciousness.

Even corporations use drumming to achieve greater efficacy. For example, Johnson reported that drumming activities increased collaboration and inspired positive relationships at Toyota (Stevens, 2007). While the experience and self reports of numerous drumming teambuilding facilitators emphasize the collaborative effectiveness of drumming exercises, there is little data reported in the literature detailing the exact effects of drumming in the international workplace. Regardless of the amount of data collected, we know that the human community has enjoyed rhythmic playing throughout time (Turow, 2005). Often facilitators have only to reference their own websites and marketing material to describe and verify the benefits of their programs.

Though effects of rhythmic drumming have a historical precedence, considering shamanism healing has been practiced in at least 47 societies (Turow, 2005), quantitative and qualitative cross-cultural data from research on the effects of drumming for organizational synergy is needed to validate the practice. So adding to the body of research on drumming, entrainment, task related communication, and efficacy may help folks explain the validity of their methodology. We can also draw from related research published on effects of drumming on political reconciliation (Slachmijlder, 2005); drug addiction treatment therapy (Winkelman, 2003), student outreach (Pfander & Williams, 2006); post-traumatic stress disorder (Bensimon et al., 2007), fatigue and mood states (Bittman et al., 2004); facing cancer (Bittman et al., 2001); and music therapy (Daveson & Skewes, 2002).

Socio-Rhythmic Entrainment

Rhythm is one of the most stable elements of culture. Music, perceived through our own unique reference fields, is always social (Clayton, Sage, and Will, 2004). Though few scientific studies have been found on the direct subject of cross-cultural entrainment of group rhythmic drumming exercises, cross-cultural and ethnomusicology research indicates that it should be important to understand cultural differences in rhythm mechanics when creating a cross-cultural rhythm entrainment exercise. A drumming facilitator, for instance, should investigate the ethnomusicology of a group's members before conducting activities so as not to disengage or marginalize a participant thereby widening the cross-cultural divergence of the group rather than melding it. Attentional dynamics and synergistic cultural techniques should be devised such that participants can equivocally attend to the rhythm (Large & Jones, 1999).

Cultural groove varies with culture. Thus the synchronization modes riding the socialization fringe vary with culture. Enculturated listeners attend more to rhythms within the framework of their culture (Clayton, Sage, & Will, 2004). Differentiation in rhythmic entrainment found in musicology can be traced to biomechanics: people walk in rhythmic styles influenced by cultural factors; individuals from different societies tend to move in different metrical signatures (Clayton, Sager, & Will, 2004). Rhythmic style shapes cultural tradition (Lomax, 1982). There are distinguishable timing and rhythm characteristic within each culture (Sadakata, Ohgushi, & Desain, 2004). Individuals in different societies more readily entrain to different biometrical patterns (Clayton, Sage, & Will, 2004). For example, while cautioning not to generalize too much, Clayton et al. find that the roots of musical rhythm can be seen in the bodily motions of Africans who walk in a poly rhythmic style moving arms and legs to different meters and contrasted with a Oriental rhythmic walking style having a steady beat in the legs while arms do a free meter melody. Each society's groove can be understood as a socio-rhythmic entrainment to a preferred organization of synchronicity.

Diversity of Rhythmic Perception

Music acts as an aural Rorschach, in that gestalt principles impose form and meaning unique to the individual that are not explicitly provided by the context (Jackson; 1998). Anacrusis, i.e. a rhythm having an unstressed note at the beginning of a phrase, provides and interesting example. Western ears perceive the anacrusis even when it is absent from the song; a perception no doubt not overlooked by a Native American or Latin ear (Stevens, 2004). Given the implications of the influence of cultural factors on participants' ability to attune to the rhythm, a researcher or facilitator must investigate and integrate the relevant culturally associated temporal structures into the design and planning of any cross-cultural rhythm based activity.

Facilitators knowledgeable of cross-cultural effects, incorporate ethnomuscial intelligence in the design and preparation of cross-cultural drumming events so as to not cause disparity and diversion among group participants. For example, imagine a participant with a dominantly European music encultured background having difficulty with the cognitive and motor demands of an African polyrhythm. He may be perceived as aloof, disinterested, or incapable. A facilitator should be aware of how culturally diverse metric groupings are articulated and engage the group in balancing activities.

Native American rhythm is based on the beating of the heart; a large drum resounds resonant biorhythms (Stevens, 2004). Western rhythm is known for its precise timing, and equal spacing of sub-beats as mathematical fractions of precisely defined measure which is generally attributed as a consequence of the graphical notation using bars contrived by 17th Century composers (Stevens, 2004). Indian rhythm is generally built of an intricate weave of cycles and epicycles, with major cycles extending as long as 512 beats (Jackson, 1998). Polyrhythms of African origin often consist of separate rhythmic streams which create the entrainment effects heard in ceremonial ritual (Stevens, 2004).

When we play, we do not want to marginalize or out-group any participants (van der Dennen, 1985); rather, we want to engage in reflective, compassionate play (Stevens, 2003). Kalani (2004) suggests that we facilitate cross-cultural synergy through inclusion, cooperation and appreciation. We can create a sense of inclusion, unity, and security by letting each participant know there is no wrong way of playing; we should help participants to feel at ease, valued and involved. With the participants' bodies, spirits and minds engaged, resonance flows.

Kalani suggests we can draw parallels between our drumming experience and analogous roles we perform in life. When we drum, we sculpt and project influences as rhythmic archetypes. During drumming we amplify some of those frequencies, find new ones, and feel the resonant awareness of a broader spectrum. A state of unified whole brain functioning, called hemispheric synchronization can be achieved with the influence of rhythmic sound (Oster, 1973). During hemispheric synchronization, the mind is more lucid, creative, intuitive (Oster) and vigilant (Lane et. al, 1997).

The state of resonance opened by somatic and psychic rhythms creates the fields that, like through the transcendent interferometer, dance their path through *where the fringes go*. Drumbeat fringe spills, surges, and barrels on Flatland reef.

PART 3: DRAW

*Pick something out there
and head for it.*

John, sailing navigation.

I hope my absence doth neglect no great designs, which by my presence might have been concluded. Shakespeare; Richard II Act III

CHAPTER 9: PROJECTIVE DRAWING IN PSYCHOLOGY

Thus a living picture emerges, containing pretty well everything that moves upon the checkerboard of the world, the good and the bad, the fair and the foul. C. G. Jung

Archaeologists and anthropologists create pictorial keys that classify symbolic meanings of ancient petroglyphs and pictographs. Symbols of idolatry, gender, purpose, action, and personality found in modern day graphics are reminiscent of early rock art. That researchers can, in general agree on some symbolic meaning of the early pictographs and extract archetypal constructs, leads one to believe that archetypal constructs can be extracted from today's drawings. Images projected from ancient myths and parables to modern day art and even business use cases are influenced by the individual and collective mindset. If you chiseled your flat-stanely-numen in the reef, what would the indigenous watermen say about your shadow; your surge, swell and spill upon the reef; the irrevocable impact of your existence?

• • •

The Drawing Relationships and Activities for Work-groups (DRAW), DRAW-Processes (DRAW-P), DRAW-Computer (DRAW-C), and DRAW-Processes-Computer (DRAW-PC) are developed here as language independent instruments (Peterson, 2009) to investigate answers to that question.

We project our shadow, fringe, and center in our drawings. Psychologists use drawing to see those projections. Projective drawing measures used in psychology are discussed next to provide insight into ways researchers identify constructs emerging from projective drawings. Then the DRAW directives will be introduced followed by a first iteration qualitative analysis of data intended to elicit your feedback.

• • •

Since the early ages of cave drawings, collections of symbols have been woven into drawings as a means to project thoughts that were otherwise verbally inexpressible. Graphical languages use collections of symbols and images to construct messages with spatial and temporal vibrancy. Today, at every turn graphical constructs convey messages such as danger, boundaries, and expected actions. Drivers follow universally acknowledged traffic icons. Ships are navigated through international waters following boundaries given by geographical information systems. Engineers communicate using contemporary, symbolic, modeling languages. Psychologists use drawing to gain a better projection of state of mind than can be revealed by people attempting to express themselves in words (Abraham, 1990).

Personality types are often described with spatial and temporal metaphors. Intuitive people are described as visionary and preferring the big picture (Boyd & Brown, 2005; Craig, Duncan, & Francis, 2006), whereas people with sensation oriented personalities are described in temporal terms, preferring sequences and logical flow (Craig et al.; Goby, 2006).

Drawing gives individuals a better avenue than words for expressing their thoughts, feelings, and underlying concerns (Peterson & Hardin, 1997). Drawings are less threatening and allow a way to express suppressed emotional pain or unspoken secrets (Malchiodi, 2002). When children, adolescents, or adults feel vulnerable or fear retaliation, drawings can help externalize emotions and ideas that they otherwise could not describe (Peterson & Hardin, 1997).

Researchers and clinicians use drawings to reveal quickly important intellectual and emotional information that may not be presented through conventional psychological testing (Malchiodi, 2002). Drawing provides an enlarged framework for individuals to construct their inner world, putting symbolic meanings to their experiences; self-expression through drawing communicates tangible, illustrative ideas for coping with everyday problems (Oster & Crone, 2004). If asked directly to verbalize emotions regarding group relationships, an individual may suppress actual feelings and deliver carefully selected verbiage congruent with an expectation, culture, or a defensive posture. Fear of retribution may cause a person to withhold information about conflicts and concerns. Drawings provide an indirect palette for discussing confrontational issues that otherwise would be hidden or elusive in the verbal process (Oster & Crone).

Projective Drawing Used in Art Therapy

Much like the way anthologists learn to find out about people through ancient drawings, art therapists learn to communicate with people to find out about their inner world through art. Though art has been used to communicate peoples' inner world since ancient days, the actual field of art therapy was considered first developed by Naumberg (1966), who used free association and interpretation with spontaneous artwork. Rhyne (1973) developed art therapy in the humanistic movement, emphasizing art activities for self-expression and group interaction. Standards of practice and ethical considerations for art therapy have been established by the American Art Therapy Association.

Clinical techniques using drawing for assessment inquire about the clients' own interpretation of their drawings, instead of imposing the views of the clinician (Naumburg, 1987). Much like a personality type assessment, confirming or disconfirming the assessment is an imperative part of the technique. It is important for users of drawing projective methodologies to consider the technique of confirming or disconfirming qualitative inferences with participants.

Art therapists have constructed developmental scoring systems for children's drawings based on sequential stages of artistic development (Leibowitz, 1999; Oster & Crone, 2004;

Williams, Fall, Eaves, & Woods-Groves, 2006). Kellogg (1970) collected and examined nearly a million drawings from children looking for common images and structures.

Researchers have documented the use of drawings for assessing personality, cognitive development, and emotional characteristics (Leibowitz, 1999; Oster & Crone, 2004; Williams et al., 2006). Some notable examples are that intellectual status can be assessed by counting the number of details in a drawing and that emotion can be assessed by observation of expansiveness or constriction in the drawing (Wadeson, 1980). Highly defensive individuals create monotonous reproductions; religious themes are often portrayed in drawings by schizophrenics; and eyes, windows, and televisions often appear in the drawings of individuals experiencing paranoia (Wadeson). Exaggerated attention or extra detail to a particular body part indicates an overdeveloped concern in that area (Reynolds & Hickman, 2004).

Clock-Drawing Test

Because visuo-spatial deficits are an early sign of dementia, researchers have investigated the use of projective clock-drawing tests as a screening for the detection of delirium, dementia, and cognitive dysfunction associated with Parkinson's disease (Emre, Aarsland, & Albanese, 2004), Alzheimer's disease (Agrell & Dehuln, 1998; Ferrucci, Cecchi, & Guralnik, 1996; Lee & Lawlor, 1995; Shulman, Gold, Cohen, & Zucchero, 1993), and hospice patients (Henderson, 2007). The clock-drawing test has a high correlation with the Mini-Mental State Examination (Ferrucci et al.; H. Lee & Lawlor) in patients with various cognitive dysfunctions. In the clock-drawing test administration, the subject is asked to draw a clock from memory; the scoring is then a count of the number of digits in the correct quadrant of the drawing (Watson, Arfken, & Birge, 1993). Thus, it is a quickly administered, nonthreatening means to provide a quantitative dementia screening metric (Agrell & Dehuln).

Human Figure Drawings

Human figure drawings are useful to psychologists as a means of assessing cognitive abilities (Williams et al., 2006). A number of tests using person drawings have been developed as projective indicators of personality (Goodenough, 1926; Harris, 1963; Koppitz, 1968; Naglieri, 1988; Reynolds & Hickman, 2004).

Research has not shown a definitive correlation between specific constructs observed in the human figure drawings and definite abnormal personality traits (Hammer, 1997). Anxieties, conflicts, and attitudes are communicated through signs and symbols that are unique to the client; therefore, a meaningful diagnosis of abnormal behavior cannot be made from indicators taken out of context (Williams et al., 2006). The following review of emergent constructs found in the literature on human figure drawings will discuss projective drawing techniques used in diagnostic processes.

Draw-a-Person Test

The Goodenough (1926) Draw-a-Man Test was the first use of human figure drawings as a projective test for assessing intelligence. The Draw-a-Man Test instructs a child to draw a picture of a man. The child's drawing is then analyzed along 51 scoring items to relate intelligence with the quality of the drawing in terms of the accuracy and number of details. Now called Draw-a-Person, the tests are primarily used as a measure of cognitive ability (Machover, 1952), indicators of emotional status (Koppitz, 1969, 1984), indicators of self-concept (Tharinger & Stark, 1990), and more recently to provide insight into personality (Williams et al., 2006).

Machover (1952) hypothesized that certain expressions in the Draw-a-Person Test provided indicators of personality characteristics. The construction of the body parts are considered to contain suggestion of social balance and control of bodily impulses; and arms and legs are symbols of social adaptation (Machover). Intense emotions are projected in the drawing as glaring eyes, bared teeth, and presence of weapons (Hammer, 1997). Bizarre, nonhuman features as well as mysterious or religious symbols suggest poor reality testing (Hammer, 1997).

Machover's adaption of the Draw-a-Person Test instructs the client to draw a person; after the first drawing, the client is instructed to draw a person of the opposite gender. The majority of individuals' first drawing is of their own gender (Machover).

Harris (1963) expanded the Goodenough Draw-a-Man to include a drawing of a man, women, and of the self. The Goodenough-Harris Drawing Test used a 12-point quality scale along 73 scoring items for the drawing of the man and 71 scoring items for the drawing of the woman; scoring was indeterminate for the self picture.

Koppitz's (1968) human-figures drawing method asked a child to draw one whole figure of a person. Koppitz analytically interpreted the drawing along 30 specific indicators summed to determine a maladjustment score. Missing features indicated maladjustment, and inclusion of unusual items indicated superior mental ability or abnormal concern with the area of the body overemphasized. Naglieri's (1988) human-figures drawing method used the three drawings of the Goodenough-Harris model with an improved scoring system along 14 criteria and an expanded norm group.

Reynolds and Hickman's (2004) Draw-A-Person Intellectual Ability Test for Children, Adolescents, and Adults (DAP: IQ) is a single drawing test used to estimate IQ. DAP:IQ scoring consists of 23 criteria identified for scoring body parts, clothing, and accessories. Internal consistency and interscorer reliability of the DAP:IQ as reported by Reynolds and Hickman was confirmed by Williams et al. (2006). The DAP:IQ single drawing test is relatively easy to administer and useful as a quick screening device for individual or group administration (Williams et al.).

Standardization samples for the Draw-a-Person Test are used to contextualize individual signs of the drawings; for example, the omission of eyes is associated with unwillingness to interact with the environment (Naglieri & Pfeiffer, 1992). In addition to interpreting individual signs, the number of times a recurring construct is repeated in a drawing can be quantified and correlated with disturbances (Koppitz, 1969, 1984).

Draw-a-Person Test reliability and validity are dependent on the psychometric qualities used to interpretive the drawing and comparisons with national norms (Koppitz, 1969, 1984; Naglieri, McNeish, & Bardos, 1991). The Draw-a-Person Test interpretation scheme is based on the following three criteria: (a) Make interpretations based on constructs that differentiate between normal and deviant characteristics, (b) the frequency of reoccurring constructs should be compared with the normal sample, and (c) effects of age should be considered in the evaluation (Koppitz, 1984). Koppitz used 30 emotional indicators to differentiate children with emotional disorders from a normal sample. The sample represents the normal population on 1-year age intervals, gender, geographic region, socioeconomic status, and ethnicity (Naglieri et al.).

House-Tree-Person Test

Buck's (1948) House-Tree-Person psychological projective test instructs a person to draw a house, a tree, and a person on separate sheets of paper. The instruction sequence is always the same, and no additional instruction is given (c.f., Hammer, 1958, 1969; Oster & Crone, 2004). Emotional indicators are then interpreted from the details of each drawing. For example, DiLeo (1983) associated the presences of a chimney on the house with nurturance and support. Moderate smoke drawn from the chimney indicates warmth and affection; a great deal of smoke drawn indicates household tension (DiLeo). The tree drawing, being least connected to home or self, is thought to be related to perceived environmental reinforcement, from which interpretations describe biographical situations and personal characteristics of the client (Oster & Crone). For example a very large tree indicates aggressive tendencies; a very small tree indicates feeling of inferiority (Bolander, 1977).

Fokunishi et al. (2002) used a modified version of the House-Tree-Person drawing test to examine the association between pretransplant and posttransplant psychiatric disorders in living-related transplantation in 31 living-related liver-transplant pairs and 65 living-related kidney-transplant pairs. The administrator using the House-Tree-Person technique asks the patient to place the house, tree, and person on the same page and in some type of action (Fokunishi et al.). This test was designed to place less burden on the recipients and donors, because it requires only one drawing (Fokunishi et al.). Fokunishi et al. found that a truncated tree drawing that lacked the upper part of the tree trunk was produced significantly more postoperatively and that a chi-square test showed significance between donors and recipients.

Draw-a-Family Test

The Draw-a-Family technique, originally given by Appel in 1931 and later expanded by Wolff in1942, asks the participant to draw a picture of his or her whole family (Oster & Crone, 2004). If names are not spontaneously noted for each family member on the drawing, the participant is asked to identify them afterward. The drawings reveal interpersonal relationships, often expressed by the relative size and placement of the family members and by substitutions or exaggeration (Harris, 1963).

Kinetic Family Drawing

Burns and Kaufman (1972) introduced the Kinetic Family Drawing test as a projective measure of perception of the dynamics of one's family by adding the directive to draw the family doing something together and by explicitly directing the individual to include themselves in the picture. The Kinetic Family Drawing test is usually administered after the Draw-a-Family test so as not to influence whether the clients leave themselves out of the Draw-a-Family drawing (Oster & Crone, 2004). The test, pertinent with children and adults, sometimes elicits the response that the family does not do anything together or shows a passive posture such as watching television (Oster & Crone). A common response shows the family at the dinner table; a lack of food present on the table indicates concerns regarding emotional nurturance (Oster & Crone). Kinetic Family Drawing can give insight into compelling interpersonal dynamics, such as when children draw themselves in proximity to parents to express status over siblings or when children represent dominance or ineffectiveness by drawing inaccurate proportions (Hammer, 1997). Facial expression in the drawings indicates whether the client perceives the family member as gentle, supportive, or harsh (Oster & Crone).

Burns and Kaufman (1972) explained that drawing constructs can indicate how affection is organized in the family, qualities of individual family members, and relationships within the family from drawings obtained from normal children as well as troubled children. Confirming that constructs can be identified from the drawings of individuals that fall within a normal characterization is import to studies concerned with normal characteristics rather than particularly deviant characteristics.

Tharinger and Stark (1990) compared qualitative and quantitative methods of scoring the Draw-a-Person Test and the Kinetic Family Drawing test. They reported that the qualitative and quantitative scoring methods significantly correlated with self-reported family functioning when the emotional indicator constructs given by Reynolds (1978) were used.

Family-Centered Circle Drawing

Burns (1990) developed the Family-Centered Circle Drawing test that uses a series of family drawings within a large circle drawn on the page. The directive is to draw a large circle on the page; then, the client draws his or her mother in the center of the circle and symbols associated with her around the periphery of the circle. The instructions are repeated for two more pictures of the father and then the self. One more drawing is done of the parents with the client together in the circle. Observations are made as to the types of symbols, spatial relationships between parents and clients, omissions and overemphasis on bodily parts, and facial expression.

Draw-a-Group Test

Abraham (1990) presented her approach to analysis of the projective drawings collected from adults participating in her Draw-a-Group Test, in which participants are given the instruction to "draw a group, a human group in any way you like" (p. 393). She reported four basic drawing constructs: (a) forms, (b) organization, (c) content, and (d) expressivity. Then, she used the constructs to infer qualitatively correlations with the participants' psychotherapy diagnosis. Abraham's research convinced her of such a great affinity between drawing and feelings that she asserted that drawing not only facilitates psychotherapy diagnosis, but also is the genuine, natural language of human expression.

The inner group is a construct used to describe style of participation, perceptions, and attitudes towards a group (Loscertales & Guil, 1999). Abraham's (1990) research focused on the inner-group intrapsychic structure of adults who participated in group-analytic therapy. Loscertales and Guil used Abraham's Draw-a-Group model to investigate common dimensions of inner group projected in the drawing of primary school teachers and students in Seville, Spain. Loscertales and Guil referred to general patterns composing drawings as Gestalts, assigning the need to belong to a circle, tendency to maintain order to a square, and hierarchical structure to a triangle. They described frames used as boundaries, corrections as indicators of anxiety, and links as desires to form relationships.

Object-Representation Projective Testing

Object-relations theorists interpret personality and the interpersonal functioning by revealing individuals' ability to differentiate between their own perspective and the perspective of others (Kernberg, 2001). Researchers adapted constructs from social-cognitive theory and object-relations theory to develop coding systems to provide a quantitative way to compare groups with known interpersonal pathology with groups of normal subjects on measures of object-relational and social-cognitve processes (Stuart, Western, Lohr, & Benjamin, 1990; Westen, Lohr, Silk, Gold, & Kerber, 1990). Stuart et al. applied Blatt, Brenneis, Schimek, and Glick's coding measures of object-relational maturity to compare the Rorschach responses of subjects with a diagnosis of borderline personality disorder with normal subjects on a measure of cognitive development. Westen et al. constructed an object-relations scale designed to assess complexity of perspective coordination, affective relationship paradigms, capacity for emotional investment, and understanding of social causality. Westen (1992) used these scales to understand how patients' behavior, thoughts, and feelings are distorted by motivational and defensive processes. Schultz and Selman's (1989) empirical study applied object-relations and social-cognition theories to measure how personality factors mediate behavior. Researchers use a variety of coded measures of object relations that collectively provide evidence of reliable, content-grounded construct validity, indicating constructs that reveal data about the quality of interpersonal relationships (Blatt & Lerner, 1983).

Diguer, Pelletier, and Hébert (2004) used principal-components factor analysis of object descriptions to evaluate structural and qualitative constructs of object representations along Blatt, Wiseman, Prince-Gibson, and Gatt's (1991) characteristics scales: affectionate, malevolent–benevolent, warm–cold, degree of constructive involvement, negative positive ideal, nurturing, successful, and weak–strong. Karmiloff-Smith's (1990) studies of children's drawings of nonexistent objects identified constructs that correlate with independence and sequential constraints. Karmiloff-Smith's methods have been developed further to confirm theories of representational flexibility (Berti & Freeman, 1997; Picard & Vinter, 1996; Spensley & Taylor, 1999; Zhi, Thomas, & Robinson, 1997).

Contextualized Thematic Representations of Creativity

Chen et al. (2002) contextualized scoring elements for thematic representation of cultural variations in creativity of European American and Chinese college students. Participants were asked to draw pictures titled Triangle, Rectangle, and Circle, which allowed for a wide variation of creative responses. Half of the participants were given the instruction to draw creatively; the other half was given the instruction to draw visual images in response to verbal stimuli.

The instruction stated: "We want you to make drawings that you personally find intuitively or subjectively appealing or 'right' to you" (Chen et al., p. 175). Chen et al. coded along four dimensions: (a) creativity, (b) uniqueness, (c) technical quality, and (d) liking. Additionally, each drawing was coded by independent coders according to seven categories of thematic contents: (a) simple, straightforward, or typical shapes; (b) decorated or three-dimensional shapes; (c) multiple shapes, embedded or arranged; (d) simple but meaningful shapes; (e) the shape in concrete context; (f) reflections of the shapes and unique perspectives; and (g) the shape in abstract context. Chen et al. used the thematic coding as a step toward contextualizing the features of the drawings in terms of the thematic representations of what the judges considered to be creative.

Franck Drawing Completion Test

Franck and Rosen's (1949) projective test of masculinity and femininity used 36 incomplete, simple, line drawings as stimulus to be completed by the subject. Franck and Rosen found that men tend to close off the stimulus lines, expand the lines, and emphasize angles; women tend to leave stimulus lines open, elaborate within the stimulus, and reduce sharp angles.

Milne and Greenway (2001) used the Franck Drawing Completion Test in their study of defense style in adults. Milne and Greenway categorized drawing content into constructs that they associated with specific defenses. For example, drawings that included whole humans correlated with lower defense score on humor.

Fix (2003) used the Franck Drawing Completion Test in his study of constructs of playfulness and creativity in adults. Fix's confirmatory factor analysis showed positive correlations between two adult playfulness scales and the Franck Drawing Completion Test.

However, McCarthy, Anthony, and Domino (1970) found no correlation between the masculinity and femininity scales of an abbreviated, 12-item Franck Drawing Completion Test with the personality measures of the California Psychological Inventory and Minnesota Multiphasic Personality Inventory. Use of the abbreviated version added questions to the results that would have been reduced if the full 36-item test had been scored (McCarthy et al.).

CHAPTER 10: THE DRAW DIRECTIVES

We are therefore obliged to adopt the method we would use in deciphering a fragmentary text or one containing unknown words: we examine the context.
C. G. Jung

Projective drawing directives are tools psychologists and researchers use to gather information about personality type. Many psychologists use projective drawing methods for assessing personality, cognitive development, and emotional characteristics (Leibowitz, 1999; Oster & Crone, 2004; Williams et al., 2006). Psychometric data and contextual themes emergent from projective drawing data have been coded and related to personality style (Goodenough, 1926; Harris, 1963; Koppitz, 1968; Naglieri, 1988; Reynolds & Hickman, 2004).

The DRAW Directive

The DRAW directive (Peterson, 2009) asks the participants to draw a picture or diagram of their organizational group. No instruction on how to draw the group is given; the instruction will allow the participants to use any type of object representation such as stick figures, block diagrams, whole person drawings, groups represented by geometric shapes, annotations, lists, labels, connecting lines, arrows, or any other style of drawing to represent their work group. The space for the drawing will be a typical   8.5" x 11" blank page but may be improvised as needed due to resources or materials.   After the drawing is collected, the facilitator should note any use of labels and ask the participant to add labels if they are needed to clarify ambiguities; if labels are added the facilitator should note that they were added as an after-fact.   A modification of the directive, the DRAW-C, is to use a computer generated graphic set thereby limiting construct selection and providing opportunity to gain insight into the choice and use of available symbols.

The DRAW-P Directive

The DRAW-P directive (Peterson, 2009) asks the participants to draw a picture or diagram of their organizational group or a subset of their group doing something, such as a process or an activity. No instruction on how to draw the process is given; instruction will allow the participant to use annotations and any type of object representation such as stick figures, block diagrams, whole person drawings, groups represented by geometric shapes, lists, labels, connecting lines, arrows, or any other style of drawing to represent their work group. The space for the drawing will be a typical 8.5" x 11" blank page but may be improvised as needed due to resources or materials. After the drawing is collected, the facilitator asks the participant to add labels if they are needed to clarify ambiguities; the addition of labels as an after-fact should be noted by the facilitator. A valuable modification of the directive, the DRAW-PC, is to use a computer graphic program for creating the drawing rather than a free hand drawing. This modification limits construct selection and provides an opportunity to gain insight into the choice and use of available constructs. In a quantitative regard, it simplifies analysis because construct selection can be explicitly quantified rather than qualitatively derived.

Drawing Directives Derived

The DRAW directives (Peterson, 2009) were derived by from the projective drawing techniques used in art therapy (Kellogg, 1970; Naumberg, 1966; Reynolds & Hickman, 2004; Rhyne, 1973; Wadeson, 1980; Williams et al., 2006); tests of visuo-spatial deficits used in assessment of early sign of dementia and patients with various cognitive dysfunctions (Agrell & Dehuln, 1998; Emre et al., 2004; Ferruci et al., 1996; Henderson, 2007; Lee & Lawlor, 1995; Shulman et al., 1986); human-figure drawing tests as projective indicators of personality (Goodenough, 1926; Harris, 1963; Koppitz, 1968; Naglieri, 1988; Reynolds & Hickman, 2004); projective testing for assessing intelligence (Machover, 1952), emotional status (Koppitz, 1969, 1984), self-concept (Tharinger & Stark, 1990) and personality (Williams et al., 2006); and estimated IQ (Reynolds & Hickman, 2004; Williams et al.). Projective drawing techniques are relatively easy to administer and useful as quick screening devises for individual or group administration (Williams et al.), comparisons with national norms (Koppitz, 1969, 1984; Naglieri et al., 1991), emotional indicators such as household tensions (Bolander, 1977, DiLeo, 1983; Oster & Crane, 2004), psychiatric disorders (Fokunishi et al., 2002), family dynamics (Burns & Kaufman, 1972), group dynamics (Abraham, 1990; Loscertales & Guil, 1999), object-relational and social-cognitve processes (Blatt & Lerner, 1983; Schultz & Selman, 1989; Stuart et al., 1990; Westen, 1992; Westen et al., 1990), representational flexibility (Berti & Freeman, 1997; Karmiloff-Smith, 1990; Picard & Vinter, 1996; Spensley & Taylor, 1999; Zhi et al., 1997), cultural variations in creativity (Chen et al., 2002), projective testing of masculinity and femininity (Franck & Rosen, 1949; McCarthy et al., 1970; Milne & Greenway, 2001), and collaboration style (Salter & Junco, 2007; Tucker, 2008).

Qualitative emergent-theory analysis of the DRAW data is encouraged. Data compiled from numerous studies can then be explored and related in subsequent qualitative and quantitative research. One challenge of emergent-theory, qualitative research is to allow the data to reveal the constructs and theoretical correlations (Mays & Pope, 2000). Thus, a researcher should not derive constructs explicitly from the previous discussion of the literature but instead use that knowledge to prepare to recognize emerging constructs in the DRAW results. When sufficient data sets are collected and shared among the community of interested researchers, emergent constructs can be triangulated with quantitative research to establish correlations.

Occupation Influences

The literature on projective tests provides insight into ways researchers have coded evaluation systems, primarily concerned with individual and family dynamics. The DRAW projective drawing technique addresses a means to identify differences in normal individuals. Research on other projective techniques provide insight into how emerging constructs have been identified by other analysts, which is valuable background for an qualitative analyst identifying constructs emerging from DRAW projective drawing data. For example constructs associated with the Kinetic Family Drawing such as proximities, relative sizing, rotations, encapsulation, edge placement, symmetry, and stick figures (Reynolds, 1978) may emerge from the qualitative analysis of the DRAW. However, because development of the DRAW is concerned with normal personality styles projected in normal group behavior, we must also consider other typical influences such as occupation.

The tools commonly used in a person's occupation may influence choice of drawing constructs; for example, a software development professional trained to use Unified Modeling Language would likely describe a software design using the spatial and temporal constructs of that language; a musician writing music likely would be comfortable with the temporal constructs of time signatures and meters; and a lifeguard would be expected to describe changing sea states in spatial terms of boundaries. To qualitatively identify constructs emerging from projective drawing data, a qualitative analyst should be knowledgeable of typical drawing constructs used in the environments of the participants. An individual's organizational environment likely will influence his or her collaboration style (Salter & Junco, 2007; Tucker, 2008) and thus may influence the projective drawing results.

Certain personality types tend to be represented more in certain occupations (Myers et al., 2003). This is due to factors such as self-selection, stereotyped selection, environment, perceived organizational fit, attrition due to bullying, etc. People often function in environments that are in opposition to their type preference, which they may find stressful (Salter & Junco, 2007).

Dimensions of environmental types influence group interaction: extraverted environments emphasize involvement and interaction; introverted environments emphasize reflection and consideration of experiences; sensing environments focus on attention to environmental elements; intuitive environments focus on creativity and discover; thinking environments emphasize depersonalized, logical operation; and feeling environments emphasize the value of support and shared reality (Salter & Junco). Personality types emerging from qualitative analysis of the DRAW may be influenced by the participants' environmental experience. Thus, studies of the DRAW should consider selection of participants from a wide variety of organizational types when feasible.

An explanation of types of constructs that may be projected in the DRAW directives is given next for the purpose of explaining the goal of the research and is not intended to be a speculative prediction of constructs that will emerge from the data. Keeping in mind that the quality of qualitative analysis depends on constructs emergent from the data (Mays & Pope, 2000); no attempt should be made in advance to code constructs expected in the results. This is important because the goal of the present work is to encourage researchers to uncover correlations in the data from which theory may emerge, rather than the data being fit to validate proposed correlations. The following discussion is given as an example vignette of the breadth of constructs and correlations that may emerge from the qualitative analysis.

One typical way organizations represent work groups is by organizational charts, which use geometric shapes to indicate roles attached by connecting lines or arrows; names of individuals filling higher roles are sometimes listed, while names of lower level employees are omitted (Molina, 2001). DRAW analysis may reveal group drawing constructs that represent organizational hierarchy, bureaucratic organization, encapsulation, repetitive forms, power distances, faces, decorations, borders, arrows, or indicators of kinetic flow or relationships.

Personality types that typically self-select into roles that use organizational charts are thinking, judging, logical decision makers who extravert thinking, whether dominant or auxiliary, and introvert their preferred perceiving function, either sensation or intuition (Myers et al., 2003). Thus the qualitative analyst may expect to find data that shows that thinking-judging individuals use constructs found in organizational chart-type layouts to represent their work group.

Another way a person may represent a work group is by spatial arrangement, where work group members are drawn as they typically are situated in a geographic or cultural relationship to each other. According to Shipman et al. (2001), people who share a workspace create visual representations of organizational communication. Thus the qualitative analyst may expect to find that individuals who working in geographically dispersed teams use spatial segregation of geographically separated group members or may omit geographically separated members from the drawing.

Roush and Atwater (1992) reported that introverts with dominant sensation personality types had the most accurate self-perceptions of personality types; thus the qualitative analysis may reveal that these individuals accurately acutely detail themselves in group drawings. Intuitive, logical people characterized by a dominant preference for either intuition or feeling, with the other as the auxiliary function, and are often described as big-picture idealists, concerned with inspiring others (Myers et al., 2003). Thus, the data may reveal that these individuals tend to draw the group omitting a specific self-figure. Sympathetic, friendly people are characterized by a dominant preference of either sensation or feeling, with the other as the auxiliary function (Myers et al.) and tend to select into transformational leadership roles and use the most positive reinforcement with followers (Roush & Atwater, 1992). Their drawings may show attention to facial expression.

Adaptable thinkers who introvert their thinking processes, whether dominant or auxiliary, and extravert their preferred perceiving function, either sensation or intuition, tend to have an ability to consider a broad range of facts but can have difficulty following logic shifts (Myers et al.); they are also overrepresented in the national sample in substance abuse workshops (Quenk & Quenk, 1996). Inspection of their DRAW drawings may show more frequent constructs such as afterthoughts, changing page orientations, and erasures. The data may reveal that reflective harmonizers, who introvert feeling, individualize roles. Or, perhaps, reflective individuals, who introvert their thinking, may emphasize depersonalized roles.

Adaptable realists that have self-selected in the arts may include creative details of scenery in their drawing. By contrast, realistic decision makers may supply standardized lists. These examples are given as a primer of the type of correlations that may emerge from the data. The qualitative analyst should look for diverse, emergent constructs from the qualitative analysis first before correlating with specific pre-conceptions of personality functions, orientations, or groupings of functions and orientations.

CHAPTER 11: DRAW STUDY

The conscious mind allows itself to be trained like a parrot, but the unconscious does not—which is why S.t. Augustine thanked God for not making him responsible for his dreams. C. G. Jung

Here is a dataset collected using the DRAW directive. These 8 drawings are presented here with discussion from the first iteration of my qualitative analysis of DRAW data. Notice that the drawings printed herein have proper names obscured. I encouraged you to perform your independent iterative deductive and inductive analysis of the presented data. I welcome your feedback!

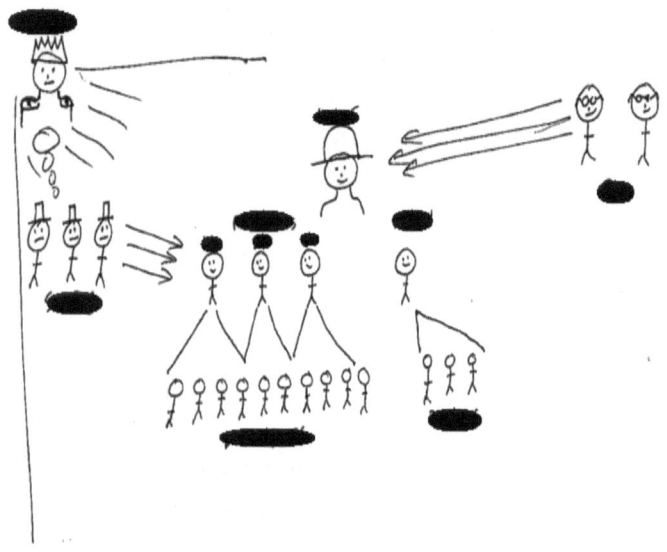

Drawing 1

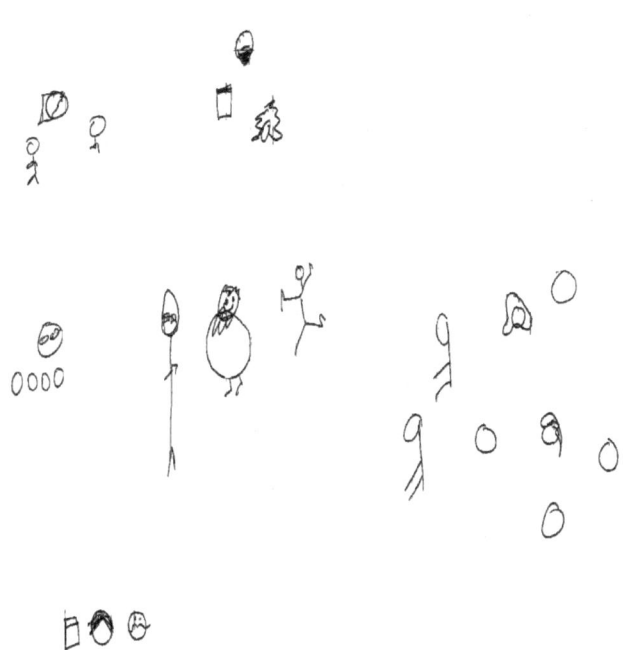

Drawing 2

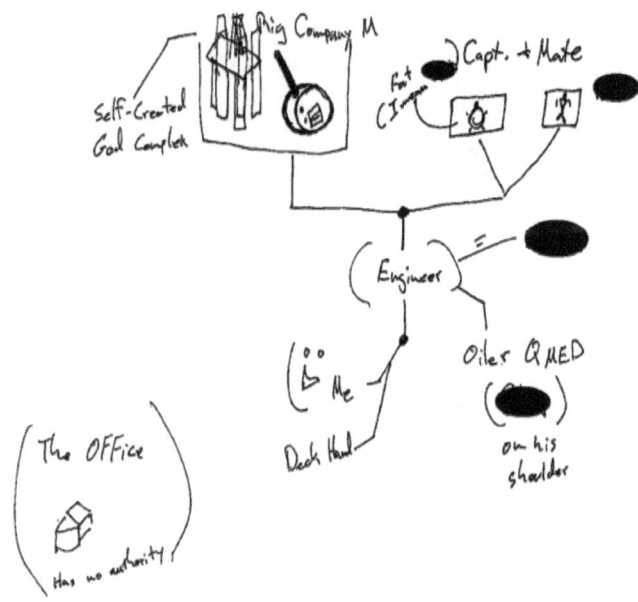

Drawing 3

Drawing 4

Objective

Jung's (1923) contrast of the introvert and extrovert emphasized elements of irrational subjectivity and rational objectivity. Introverts withdrawing libido from object; extroverts placing such a grand importance that even the subjective is oriented to the object, the importance of which ever increasing. The crown in Drawing 1 places importance on a an individual. Of course in reality the person probably does not wear a crown; the crown was created in the subjective view of the drawer. The hats and glasses are subjective denotations of importance and roles as well. Glasses also appear in Drawing 2 along with beards and hair but in this drawing they are presumably more realistic identifiers of individual style; perhaps not as subjective as the others. An interesting note here is that after inspection, Drawer 2 said that she realized that she unintentionally drew her extroverted colleagues with front-on perspective and her introverted colleagues with side-on perspective, as if avoiding direct eye contact. This seems to indicate subjective intuiting because she drew them from her perspective and was not conscious of the fact until latter inspection. Had she indicated the attitude from the colleague's perspective, perhaps labeling them with an "I", it would be considered more objective intuiting.

The drawer of Drawing 3 was indeed so concerned with his subjective sensing perception of his colleagues that the person drawn with a round belly was labeled as "Fat" in obvious contrast to the well built co-work labeled as "Mate"; each where also labeled objectively by name (herein obscured). Extreme subjective importance is given to the "Rig Company M[an]" drawn in 3-D as an oil-drilling platform and labeled "Self-Created God Complex". Drawer 3's subjective sensual interest in body extends to the accompanying over-emphasized radio antenna.

A notable similarity of Drawings 1 and 2 is the use of repetitive, less detailed, and even paper-doll like figures representing work-group members, presumably not distinguished in the subjective vision. These repetitive constructs are absent in Drawing 3. Drawing 4 is almost exclusively repetitive stick figures drawn as if they were posing for a picture. It turns out that Drawer 4 did just that, he simple drew a reproduction of a group photo. The labels were added after the drawing was complete, at the request of the facilitator. When asked again to identify himself in the drawing,

Drawer 4 simply colored in his hair. This recreation of a photo may at first seem rather objective however consider that a subjective view point is most useful for holding and recreating images. Objective types are less likely to be guided by an internally held vision. Perhaps most significant in this drawing is that some of the stick figures are drawn side facing with both arms on one side of the body stick. Similar to Drawer 2 who inadvertently drew introverts in side view, Drawer 4 seems to have inadvertently drawn females in side view.

Drawer 1, 2, 3, & 4 included themselves in their drawing but not with objective emphasis. Drawer 3 does explicitly indicate an objective "Me" however adorned with a subjective smiley face. Drawer 3 uses a few objective labels but for the most part qualifies them with a subject comments; in one case, even including a pun with a proper name.

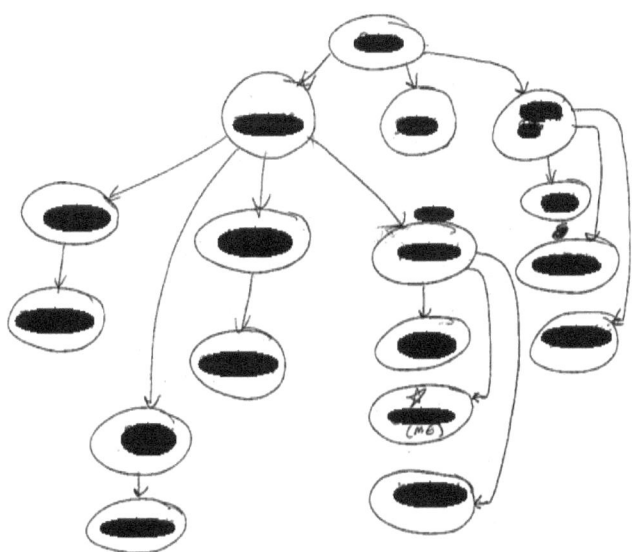

Drawing 5

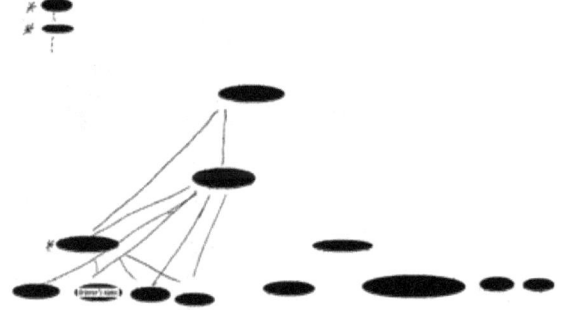

Drawing 6

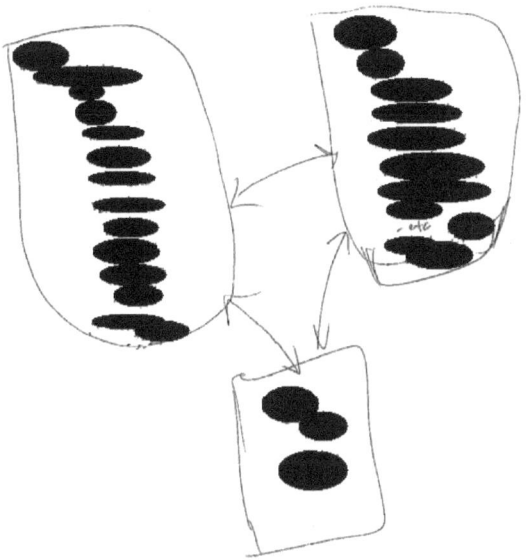

Drawing 7

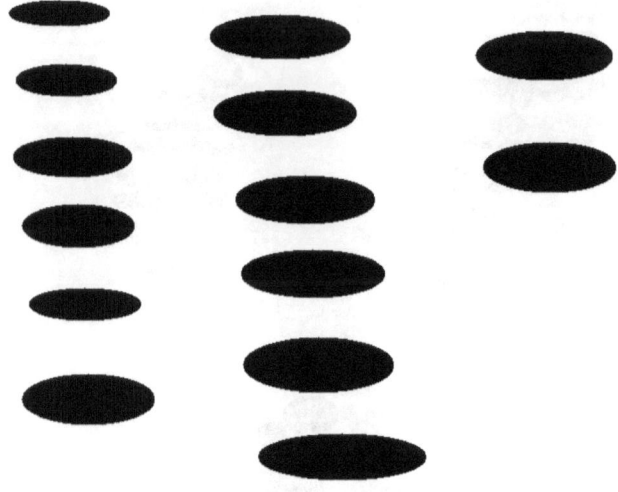

Drawing 8

Subjective

Of eight drawings in this collection, only 4 actually drew human-figure like representations of the people in their organization. The other four represented individuals by proper name or role. Drawing 5 explicitly names individuals (proper names obscured herein) with circles around each and lines connecting in a hierarchical fashion. Drawer 5 is highlighted with a star and labeled with the word "me" without prompting by the facilitator. Drawing 6 uses names and arrows in a hierarchical format; includes a self reference; but instead of highlighting himself, highlights his boss. Drawer 7 uses sub-group organizational names, circles geographically distant sub-groups, and uses arrows to indicate bi-directional connectivity rather than hierarchy. Drawer 8 simply listed names.

Certainly this latter group of Drawers 5-8 was less subjective in there expression of individuals then the former group of Drawers 1-4. Drawers 1-4's more interpretive style indicates a subjective perception of their colleagues. Drawers 5-8's explicit one-to-one labeling appears objective; no subjective interpretation is attempted in these drawings. That

Jung states that an extraverted type orients himself in accordance with the data supplied by the outside world while an introverted type orients to the subjective leads us to investigate if Drawers 1-4 are introverted types and Drawers 5-8 are extroverted types.

The literature on the introversion-extroversion dichotomy revealed that many researchers consider extroverts to be more oriented to social constructs than introverts (Francis, Craig, & Robbins, 2007; Myers et al., 2003). At least two of our objective drawers are indeed socially oriented. Notice that they used arrows to indicate group organization and hierarchy in their drawings. Thus these presumed extroverts' objective drawings are consistent with an objective – extrovert correlation.

Also, at least two of our subjective drawers report their personality types are consistent with Jung's description of the introverted type. Here again, their subjective drawings were consistent with a subjective-introvert correlation. However, at this point let's decline to hypothesize that Drawers 1-4 are introverts and Drawers 5-8 are extroverts; simply note that the former are subjective and the latter, objective. We will have to look further into the rational and irrational functions to understand subjectivity and objectivity in the introverted and extroverted attitudes.

Rational

Perceiving irrational types are oriented by the subjective and the judging rational types are oriented by the objective (Jung, 1923). Our findings so far are congruent with the notion that irrational extroverts, placing such a grand importance on objects that even the subjective is oriented to the object, project objectivity. We may then expect that rational introverts, grounded on the functions of rational judgment based on objective and subjective data, project subjectivity. Our data does not concur with this latter notion. Instead, Drawing 8 is better interpreted from the viewpoint that rational introverts, continually dealing in judgments, arouse prejudice of their own nature, and in self-detriment, adapt an untrue nature to avoid reproach. Worth noting here is that upon completing the drawing, the socially disengaged Drawer 8 said that he knew what the facilitator was looking for and so intentionally did something else.

Irrational

Sensation and intuition are the irrational functions referred to as perceiving. Irrational types are oriented by the subjective amid a flux of events; they are guided by what happens rather than by rational judgment (Jung, 1923). Objective stimulus is necessary to sensation; in the subjective it ultimately produces something different than what one may consider the reality of the external situation (Jung). Thus even the introverted sensation type is energized by external influences. "Whereas the extraverted sensation type is guided by the intensity of objective influences, the introverted type is guided by the intensity of the subjective sensation excited by the objective stimulus." (p. 255).

Drawing 3 stands out as guided by intensive subjective sensation excited by objective stimulus. Drawing 3's sensuous content is nearly palatable: A man represented as hand held radio whose antenna emerges from the page in fastidious 3-D detail. The object's reality has been alienated; left to the mercy of the subjective shadow; it plays its part in an illusory myth amid flaring ambiguities and sordid possibilities. This is consistent with the self reported introverted sensation type of Drawer 3.

In contrast, intensity of objective influence, as expected in the extraverted sensation type, is apparent in Drawing 6 which accords value to the starred individual with no sensuous content. It would seem that the judging rational function is subordinated here to sensation. Subordinating the rational to sensation may cause exhibition of negative, infantile, and archaic traits (Jung, 1923) which seems apparent in scratchiness of Drawing 6 as well. Also notable in both Drawings 3 and 6 is the repressed intuitive function where some of the individuals are floating dissociated from the picture; sensed but not integrated. The introverted sensation type's with a flagrant note.

Like sensation, intuition is guided by the subjective; the subjective being suppressed in the extravert. For the introvert, the subjective is the decisive factor; the intuitive is concerned not with external objects but with what the external has released in him. Intuition receives sensation only as the impetus to perceive an inner image (Jung, 1923). "For intuition, therefore, unconscious images acquire the dignity of things" (p. 259). The intuitive is continually seeking new possibilities and tearing down the present to be renewed by his everlasting search for change: "Introverted intuition apprehends the images arising from the a priori inherited foundations of the unconscious" (p.261). These foundations are the archetypes' experiences of all times. Thus the intensification of intuition can results in enigma and separation from tangible reality. They can become intoxicated by their inner vision. But as the conscious co-exists with the unconscious, the intuitive, through its perception of inner processes, foresee possibilities and events with prophetic foresight (Jung).

The Drawer of Drawing 2 noted after drawing that there was no significant reason for placing the 3 individuals in the center of the drawing; that they were not placed in the center as a main focus rather that she had filled the edges first which left only the center for these last 3 guys. Later, all 3 became a primary focus of the group and eventually took central roles. Drawer 2 reported as an introverted intuitive.

CHAPTER 12: EMERGENT DATA

Anyone who identifies with the collective psyche—or, in mythological terms, lets himself be devoured by the monster— and vanishes in it, attains the treasure that the dragon guards, but he does so in spite of himself and to his own greatest harm. C. G. Jung

At the 2006 IEEE Conference on System Sciences, Wu, Lin and Lin (2006) stated that theoretical foundations for virtual and face-to-face collaboration need to be strengthened. Empirical research has shown that personality factors influence collaboration (Carlyn, 1977; Shank & Langmeyer, 1994). Projective-testing methodologies and scoring systems techniques can be used to reliably and validly assess personality factors (Goodenough, 1926; Harris, 1963; Koppitz, 1968; Naglieri, 1988; Reynolds & Hickman, 2004). Thus research studies on emergent theory from interpretation of the projective drawing data will answer the call for contributions to theoretical foundations for increasing efficacy and will aid subsequent qualitative and quantitative researchers in establishing coding standardizations and methodologies for projective drawing techniques.

Past research has shown that personality dynamics influence organizational culture (Salter & Junco, 2007; Tucker, 2008). We know that workplace anxiety and defense mechanisms (Brousse et al., 2008) lead to inaccurate personality assessments (Bauer et al., 1998; Mahar et al., 1995; McFarland, 2003). We also know that projective drawing decouples those defenses and anxieties (Malchiodi, 2002). Projective drawing has been used by psychologists to study deviant personality characteristics (Coulacoglou & Kine, 1995; Dent-Brown & Wang, 2004; Edwards, 1996; Fokunishi et al., 2002; Joy & Hicks, 2004). However, an important gap remains in the literature in that we still do not have a collective database of normal personality characteristic drawing data sufficient to establish standardized methodologies and coding. Finding correlations within the normal personality-type diversity could lay the groundwork for further studies on language independent projective drawing methods for use in many diverse studies.

Future studies will build on the framework to contextualize emergent constructs across larger populations. Questions concerning how drawing constructs are interpreted by others are valuable; one practical application will help developers of an electronic collaboration tool choose symbols for a standard selection palette. Another practical application is the use of drawings in the development of a nonverbal, forced-choice inventory format for non-reading, or non-verbalizing individuals. Contributing to the emergent data has implications for positive social change by increasing validity of projective techniques to study the influence of culture, gender, and life span development. Data sets collected and shared across vast interests will mature and modernize our collective emergent theory of projective personality analysis.

PARTICIPATION

An example participation form is included in here, handy for you to begin collecting data and making notes of your own findings. After the drawer completes the drawing take note of the information relevant to your study. Here is a suggested list:

- What labels or notes, if any, were added for clarification after the drawing was completed?

- What can you note about the drawer's personality type or style? If you have a formal personality evaluation you may want to use that description. If available, attach a copy of the report.

- What is the primary function of the group that was drawn?

- Does the drawer enjoy interacting with this group?

- Does the drawer live in a predominantly individualist or collectivist society?

- What is the drawer's country of residence and primary language?

- What are the drawer's occupation, gender description, and age?

- Invite the drawer to add additional information or contact information if open to having a researcher follow up.

Consider reading Jung's work on personality types to expand your analysis. If you want quantified reports for you analysis you might use one of the many personality inventories servers available online (http://www.swellpersonality.com).

I will be most delighted if you share your findings with me. You may need to expand or customize the informed consent statement to meet your specific intent. Please remember to respect participants' confidentiality.

EXAMPLE PARTICIPATION FORM

Facilitator: _____

Informed Consent: The purpose of this study is to learn about people and drawing. You will be asked to draw your group; a brief discussion may follow. This will only take a few minutes and you may decline or withdraw at any time without any penalty. Your participation is voluntary and there is no compensation. The study is designed to fall within none to minimal risk boundaries. If you perceive a risk you should decline or withdraw. The benefits of participation are that you will contribute to the body of knowledge about people and drawing. Identifying information about you and third parties will be protected from inappropriate disclosure. Data and observations based on the data may be shared and published. Proper names will be obscured and/or re-coded if used in publication. If you are not at least 18 years old please have your parent give consent.

I voluntarily consent to participate in this study. I consent to the use and transfer of my drawing and information for research and publication.

_____date_____

❑ DRAW: Please draw your organizational group.

❑ DRAW-P: Please draw your organizational group or a subset of your organizational group doing something, such as a process or an activity.

❑ DRAW-C: Please draw your organizational group (attach computer drawing).

❑ DRAW-PC: Please draw your organizational group or a subset of your organizational group doing something, such as a process or an activity (attach computer drawing).

Use the back of this page to do your drawing or attach another sheet.

REFERENCES

Abbott, A. E. (1884). *Flatland A Romance of Many Dimensions*. NY: Dover.

Abraham, A. (1990). The projection of the inner group in drawing. *Group Analysis, 23*, 391-403.

Agrell, B., & Dehuln, O. (1998). The clock-drawing test. *Age and Ageing, 27*, 399-403.

American Psychological Association (APA) (2007). *Publication manual of the American Psychological Association (5th ed.)*. Washington, D. C.: Author.

American Psychological Association. (2002). *Ethical principles of psychologists and code of conduct*. Retrieved September 22, 2007, from http://www.apa.org/ethics/code2002.html#principle_d.

Ancona, D., & Chong, C., L., (1992). *Entrainment: Cycle and synergy in organizational behavior*. Cambridge MA: MIT.

Ballard, D. & Seibold, R. (2004). Organizational member's communication and temporal experience. *Communication Research, 31*(2), 135-172.

Ballard, M. E., Dodson, A. R., & Bazzini, D.G. (1999). Genre of music and lyrical content: Expectation effects. *The Journal of Genetic Psychology, 160*, 476-487.

Bandura, A. (2001). The changing face of psychology at the drawing of a globalization era. *Canadian Psychology, 42*(1), 12-24.

Barkley, W. (2005). Scientific Anomalies The Plasma Universe Epoch Times: retrieved from http://www.theepochtimes.com/news/5-6-1/29185.html

Bauer, T. N., Maertz, C. P., Dolen, M. R., & Campion, M. A. (1998). Longitudinal assessment of applicant reactions to employment testing and test outcome feedback. *Journal of Applied Psychology, 83*(6), 892-903.

Bensimon, M., Amir, D., & Wolf, Y. (2007) Drumming through trauma:Music therapy with post-traumatic soldiers. *The Arts in Psychotherapy, 9*(2), 1-15.

Berti, A. E., & Freeman, N. H. (1997). Representational change in resources for pictorial innovation: A three-component analysis. *Cognitive Development, 12*(4), 501-522.

Bigand, E., Vieillard, S., Madurell, F., Marozeau, J., & Dacquet, A. (2005). Multidimensional scaling of emotional responses to music: The effect of musical expertise and of the duration of excerpts. *Cognition and Emotion, 19*, 1113-1139.

Bittman, B. Berk, L., Felten, ., Westengard, J., Simonton, O., Pappas, J., Ninehouser, M. (2001). Composite effects of group drumming music therapy on modulation of neuroendocrine immune parameters in normal subjects. *Alternative Therapies, 7*(1), 38-47.

Bittman, B., B., Snyder, C., Bruhn, K., T., Liebfreid, F., Stevens, C., K., Westengard, J., & Umbacn, P., O. (2004). Recreational music-making: An integrative group intervention for reducing burnout and improving mood states in first year associate degree nursing students: Insights and economic impact. *International Journal of Nursing Education Scholarship, 1*(1), 1-26.

Blatt, S. J., & Lerner, H. (1983). The psychological assessment of object representation. *Journal of Personality Assessment, 4*, 7-28.

Blatt, S. J., Wiseman, H., Prince-Gibson, E., & Gatt, C. (1991). Object representation and change in clinical functioning. *Psychotherapy, 28*(2), 273-283.

Blood, A., Zatorre, J., Bermudez, P., & Evans, C. (1999). Emotional responses to pleasant and unpleasant music correlate with activity in the paralimbic brain regions. *Nature Neuroscience, 2*, 382-387.

Bohm, D. (1951). *Quantum Theory*. New York: Prentice Hall. 1989 reprint, New York: Dover.

Bolander, K. (1977). *Assessing personality through tree drawings*. New York: Basic Books.

Botwin, M. D. (1995). Review of the NEO-personality inventory. *Twelfth mental measurements yearbook*. Retrieved August 16, 2008, from EBSCO Mental Measurements Yearbook database.

Boyd, R., & Brown, T. (2005). Pilot study of the Myers-Briggs Type Indicator personality profiling in emergency department senior medical staff. *Emergency Medicine Australiasia, 17*, 200-203.

Brousse, G., Fontana, L., Ouchchane, L., Boisson, C., Laurent, G., Bourguet, D. Perrier, A., Schmitt, A., Llorca, P., M., & Chamoux, A. (2008). Psychopathological features of a patient population of targets of workplace bullying. *Occupational Medicine, 58* (2), 122-129.

Brown, S., Merker, B., & Wallin, N., L., (2000). An introduction to evolutionary musicology in S. Brown, B. Merker, & N. L. Wallin (Eds.). *The origins of music*. Cambridge, MA: MIT

Buck, J. N. (1948). The H-T-P Technique: A qualitative and qualitative scoring manual. *Journal of Clinical Psychology, 4,* 317-396.

Bunderson, C., Olsen, J., & Herrmann, W. (1982). A fourfold model of multiple brain dominance and its validation through correlational research. Scientific and technical report #10: General Electric. Orem. UT: Wicat Incorporated Learning Design Laboratories

Burns, R. C. (1990). *Guide to Family-Centered Circle Drawings (F-C-C-D) with symbol probes and visual free association.* New York: Brunner/Mazel.

Burns, R. C., & Kaufman, S. H. (1972). *Actions, styles and symbols in Kinetic Family Drawings (KFD): An interpretative manual.* New York: Brunner/Mazel.

Canazza, S., De Poli, G., Roda, A., & Vidolin, A. (2003). An abstract control space for communication of sensory expressive intention in music performance. *Journal of New Music Research, 32*(3), 281-294.

Carlyn, M. (1977). An assessment of the Myers-Briggs Type Indicator. *Journal of Personality Assessment, 41*(5), 461-473.

Chen, C., Kasof, J., Himsel, A. J., Greenberger, E., Dong, Q., & Xue, G. (2002). Creativity in drawing of geometric shapes: A cross-cultural examination with consensual assessment technique. *Journal of Cross-Cultural Psychology 33*, 171-189.

Clayton, M., Sager, R., & Will, U. (2004). In time with the music: The concept of entrainment and its significance for ethnomusicology. *ESEM CounterPoint, 1*, 1-45.

Collier, J., & Burch, M. (1998). Order from rhythmic entrainment and the orign of levels through dissipation. *Symmetry: Culture and Science, 9* (2), 4-19.

Coulacoglou, C., & Kine, P. (1995). The Fairy Tale Test: A novel approach in projective assessment. *British Journal of Protective Psychology, 40*(2), 10-31.

Craig, C., Duncan, B., & Francis, L. (2006). Psychological type preferences of Roman Catholic priests in the United Kingdom. *Journal of Beliefs & Values: Studies in Religion & Education, 27*(2), 157-164.

Crawley, E. J., Acker-Mills, B. E., Pastore, R. E., & Weil S. (2002). Change detection in multi-voice music: The role of musical structure, musical training, and task demands. *Journal of Experimental Psychology: Human Perception and Performance, 28*(2), 367-378.

Daveson, B. & Skewes, K., (2002). A philosophical inquiry into the role of rhythm in music therapy. *The Arts in Psychotherapy, 29*, 265-270.

Dawdy, G., N. (2006). *The social compass.* Shelbyville, KY: Wasteland Press.

Demany, L., & Semal, C. (2002). Limits of rhythm perception. *The Quarterly Journal of Experimental Psychology, 55*(A), 643-657.

Dent-Brown, K., & Wang, M. (2004). Developing a rating scale for projected stories. *Psychology and Psychotherapy, 77*(3), 325-334.

DeRidder C., G., & Wilcox, M., A.(1999). How to improve group productivity. Whole-brain teams set new benchmarks. *The Brain Connection.* 1-8

Diguer, L., Pelletier, S., & Hébert, É. (2004). Personality organizations, psychiatric severity, and self and object representations. *Psychoanalytic Psychology, 21*(2), 259-275.

DiLeo, J. H. (1983). *Interpreting children's drawings.* New York: Brunner/Mazel.

Edwards, J. (1996). Examining the clinical utility of the Moreno Social Atom Projective Test. Journal of Group *Psychotherapy, Psychodrama and Sociometry, 49*(2), 51-75.

Edwards, J., Lanning, K., & Hooker, K. (2002). The MBTI and social information processing: An incremental validity study. *Journal of Personality Assessment, 78*(3), 432-450.

Ellis, A. E. (2003). Personality type and participation in networked learning environments. *Educational Media International, 40*(1/2), 101.

Emre, M., Aarsland, D., & Albanese, A. (2004). Rivastigmine for dementia associated with Parkinson's disease. New England Journal of Medicine, 351(24), 2509-2518.

Ferrucci L, Cecchi F, Guralnik J., M., (1996). Does the clock drawing test predict cognitive decline in older persons independent of the Mini-Mental State Examination? *Journal of American Geriatric Society, 44*, 1326-1331.

Fix, G. A. (2003). The psychometric properties of playfulness scales with adolescents. Dissertation Abstracts International: Section B: *The Sciences and Engineering, 64*(2-B), 999.

Fokunishi, I., Sugawara,Y., Takayama, T., Makuuchi, M., Kawarasaki, H., & Surman, O. S. (2002). Association between pretransplant psychological assessments and posttransplant psychiatric disorders in living-related transplantation. *Psychosomatics, 43*(1), 49-54.

Foret, S., Bigand, E., & McAdams S. (2000). Divided attention in music. *International Journal of Psychology, 35*, 270-278.

Fraisse, P. (1982). Rhythm and tempo. In Deutsch, D. (Ed.), The psychology of music. Sydney: Academic Press.

Francis, L., Craig, C., & Robbins, M. (2007). The relationship between psychological type and the three major dimensions of personality. *Current Psychology, 25*(4), 257-271.

Franck, K., & Rosen, E. (1949). A projective test of masculinity-femininity. Journal of *Consulting Psychology, 13*(4), 247-256.

Frisbie, C., J. (1971). Anthropological and ethnomuscial implications of comparitive analysis of Bushmen and African Pygmy music. *Ethnology, 10*(3), 265-290.

Gagnon, L., & Peretz, I. (2003). Mode and tempo relative contributions to "happy-sad" judgments in equitone melodies. *Cognition and Emotion, 17*, 25-40.

Goby, V. P. (2006). Personality and online/offline choices: MBTI profiles and favored communication modes in a Singapore study. *CyberPsychology & Behavior, 9*(1), 5-13.

Goodenough, F. (1926). *Measurement of intelligence by drawings.* Chicago: World Book.

Graham, R. (2007). Music as socio emotional confluence: A comment of Bispham. *Music Perception, 25*(2), 167-168.

Green B. R. (2003). *The Elegant Universe: Superstrings, Hidden Dimensions, and the Quest for the Ultimate Theory.* New York: W. W. Norton & Company, Inc.

Hammer, E. (1997). *Advances in projective drawing interpretation.* Springfield, IL: Charles C. Thomas.

Hammer, E. F. (1958). *The clinical application of figure drawings.* Springfield, IL: Charles C. Thomas.

Hammer, E. F. (1969). Hierarchal organization of personality and the H-T-P, achromatic and chromatic. In J. N. Buck & E. F. Hammer (Eds.), *Advances in the House-Tree-Person technique: Variations and applications* (pp. 1-35). Los Angeles: Los Angeles Western Psychological Services.

Harris, D. B. (1963). *Children's drawings as measures of intellectual maturity.* New York: Harcourt, Brace, & World.

Hart, M. (1991). Rhythm as a tool for healing and health in the aging process. Testimony Before the U.S. Senate Committee on Aging. Retrieved January 12, 2008, from

http://www.mickeyhart.net/Pages/senspeech.
html

Hawking, S., W., & Penrose, R. (1994). *The nature of space and time*. Princeton: Princeton, NJ: University Press.

Henderson, M. (2007). Use of the clock-drawing test in a hospice population. *Palliative Medicine, 21*(7), 559-565.

Hermann, N. (1996). *The whole brain business book.* NY: McGraw-Hill.

Hogan, J. P. (2007). Flexible Thinking & Cosmic Electricity Lecture and accompanying notes retrieved from: http://www.jamesphogan.com/talks/Eglin_FT CE.pdf

Honing, H. (2006). On the growing role of observation, formalization and experimental method in musicology. *Empirical Musicology Review, 1*(1), 2-6.

Howell, S. H. (2004). Students' perception of Jesus personality as assessed by Jungian-Type inventories. *Journal of Psychology and Theology, 32*(1), 50-58.

Hull, A. (1998). *Drum circle spirit facilitating human potential through rhythm.* Incline Village, NV: White Cliffs Media, Inc.

Hyson, M. T. (2003). Dolphins, therapy and autism. Sirius Institute. Retrieved January 10, 2008, from http://www.planetpuna.com/dolphin-paper/Dolphin-Paper.pdf

Iyer, V. (2003) Embodied minde, situtated cognition, and expressive microtiming in African-American music. *Music Perception, 19*(3), 387-414.

Jackson, W., H. (1998). Cross-cultural perception and structure of music. Organizational Learning & Instructional Technologies. Albuquerque, NM: University of New Mexico.

Jalife, J. (1984). Mutual entrainment and electrical coupling as mechanisms for synchronous firing of rabbit sino-atrial pace maker cells. *Journal of Physiology, 356*, 221-243.

Jenkins, F. A. & White, H. E. (1976). *Fundamentals of Optics*. New York: McGraw-Hill.

Jeong, J., Joung, M. K., & Kim, S. Y. (1998). Quantification of emotion by nonlinear analysis of the chaotic dynamics of electroencephalograms during perception of 1/f music. Biol. *Cybern. 78*, 217-225.

Johnson, R., J., (2003) American music conference. Retrieved January 8, 2008, from http://www.massdrumming.com/drumscience.html

Joy, S., & Hicks, S., (2004). The need to be different: Primary trait structure and impact on projective drawings. *Creativity Research Journal, 16*(2), 331-339.

Jung, C. G. (1955). Mandalas. (Du Trans), Zurich.

Jung, C. G. (1960). *Synchronicity.* (R. F. C. Hull, Trans.). Princeton: Bollingen Series Princeton University Press.

Jung, C. G. (1976). Aion: Phenomenology of the Self. In J. Campbell (Ed.) (R. F. C. Hull, Trans.), *The Portable Jung.* New York: Penguin Books. (Original work published 1951).

Jung, C. G. (1976). The Transcendent Function. In J. Campbell (Ed.) (R. F. C. Hull, Trans.), *The Portable Jung.* New York: Penguin Books. (Original work 1916 first published 1953).

Jung, C. G. (1976). Psychological Types. In J. Campbell (Ed.) (R. F. C. Hull, Trans.). *The Portable Jung.* New York: Penguin Books. (Original work published 1923).

Jung, C. G. (1976). Dream Symbolism in Relation to Alchemy. In J. Campbell (Ed.) (R. F. C. Hull, Trans.), *The Portable Jung.* New York: Penguin Books. (Original work published 1944).

Juslin, P. N., & Laukka, P. (2004). Expression, perception and the induction of musical emotions: A review and a questionnaire study of everyday listening. *Journal of New Music Research, 33*(3), 217-238.

Kalani (2004). *Together in rhythm.* Los Angles: Alfred Publishing.

Karagiannidis, C., & Sampson, D. (2002). Accommodating learning styles in adaptation logics for personalised learning systems. In P. Barker & S. Rebelsky (Eds.), Proceedings of World Conference on Educational Multimedia, Hypermedia and Telecommunications 2002 (pp. 1715-1726). Chesapeake, VA: Association for the Advancement of Computing in Education.

Karmiloff-Smith, A. (1990). Constraints on representational change: Evidence from children's drawing. *Cognition, 34*(1), 57-83.

Kellogg, R. (1970). *Analyzing children's art.* Palo Alto, CA: Mayfield.

Kennedy, R., & Kennedy, D. (2004). Using the Myers-Briggs Type Indicator in career counseling. *Journal of Employment Counseling, 41*(1), 38-44.

Kernberg, O. F. (2001). Object relations, affects, and drives: Toward a new synthesis. *Psychoanalytic Inquiry, 21*(5), 604-619.

Keyser, J. D. & Klassen, M. (2001) *Plains Indian Rock Art*. Washington Press.

Koppitz, E. M. (1968). *Psychological evaluation of children's human figure drawings*. New York: Grune & Stratton.

Koppitz, E. M. (1984). *Psychological evaluation of human figure drawings by middle school pupils*. Orlando, FL: Grune & Stratton.

Koppitz, E. M. (1969). Emotional indicators on human figure drawings of boys and girls from middle class backgrounds. *Journal of Clinical Psychology, 25*(4), 432-434.

Krumhansl, C. L. (2002). Music: A link between cognition and emotion. *Current Directions in Psychological Science, 11*(2), 45-50.

Lane, J., D., Kasian, S., J., Owens, J., E., & Marsh, G. R. (1997). Binaural auditory beats affect vigilance performance and mood. *Physiology & Behavior, 63*(2), 249-252

Large, E., W. & Jones, M., R.(1999). The dynamics of attending: How people track time-varying events. *Psychological Review, 106*(1), 119-159.

Lee, H., & Lawlor, L. H. (1995). State-dependent nature of the clock drawing task in geriatric depression. *Journal of American Geriatrics Society, 43*, 796-798.

Leibowitz, M. (1999). *Interpreting projective drawings: A self psychological approach.* New York: Brunner/Mazel.

Letiche, H. & Hagemeijer, R. E. (2004). Linkages and entrainment. *Journal of Organizational Change Management 17*(4), 365-382.

Lilienfeld, S. O., Wood, J. M., & Garb, H. N. (2000). The scientific status of projective techniques. *Psychological Science in the Public Interest, 1*(2), 27-66.

Lindstrom, E. (2003). The contribution of immanent and performed accents to emotional expression in short tone sequences. *Journal of New Music Research, 32*(3), 269-280.

Loscertales, F., & Guil, A. (1999). Teacher's inner group and professional identity: A study based on the DAG model. *Group Analysis, 32,* 349-366.

Macdaid, G. P., McCaulley, M. H., & Kainz, R. I. (2005). *Atlas of type tables.* Gainsville, FL: Center for Applications of Psychological Type.

Machover, K. (1952). *Personality projection in the drawing of the human figure.* Springfield, IL: Charles C. Thomas.

Maclean (1952) The limbic system ("visceral brain") in relation to central gray and reticulum of the brain stem. Evidence of interdependence in emotional processes. *Psychosomatic Medicine, 5*, 354-366.

Madison, G. Experiencing groove induced by music: Consistency and phenomenology. *Music Perception, 24*(2), 201-208.

Mahar, D., Cologon, J., & Duck, J. (1995). Response strategies when faking personality questionnaires in a vocational selection setting. *Personality and Individual Differences, 18*(5), 605-609 .

Malchiodi, C. A. (Ed.). (2002). *Handbook of art therapy*. New York: Guilford Press.

Maxfield, M. (2006). Effects of rhythmic drumming on EEG and subjective experience. *Interdisciplinary Research and Clinical Perspectives*. Palo Alto, CA: Stanford University.

Mays, N., & Pope, C. (2000). Assessing quality in qualitative research. *British Medical Journal, 320*(7226), 50-52.

McCarthy, D., Anthony, R. J., & Domino, G. (1970). A comparison of the CPI, Franck, MMPI, and WAIS masculinity-femininity indexes. *Journal of Consulting and Clinical Psychology, 35*(3), 414-416.

McCaulley, M. H. (1990). The Myers-Briggs Type Indicator: A measure for individuals and groups. *Measurement and Evaluation in Counseling and Development, 22,* 181-195.

McFarland, L. A. (2003). Warning against faking on a personality test: Effects on applicant reactions and personality test scores. *International Journal of Selection and Assessment, 11*(4), 265-276.

McGrath, J. E. & Kelly, J., R. (1986). *Time and human interaction: toward a social psychology of time.* New York: Guilford Press.

McNeil, W. (1995). *Keeping it in time: Dane and drill in human history.* Cambridge, MA: Harvard University Press.

Meneely, J., & Portillo, M.(2005). The adaptable mind in design: relating personality, cognitive style, and creative performance. *Creativity Research Journal, 17*(2),155-166.

Milne, L. C., & Greenway, P. (2001) Drawings and defense style in adults. *The Arts in Psychotherapy, 28*(4), 245-249.

Molina, J. L. (2001). The informal organizational chart in organizations: An approach from the social network analysis. *Connections, 24*(1), 78-79.

Myers, I. B., McCaulley, M. H., Quenk, N. L., & Hammer, A. L. (2003). *MBTI manual: A guide to the development and use of the Myers-Briggs Type Indicator* (3rd ed.). Mountainview, CA: CPP.

Myers, I.B., & McCaulley, M.H. (1985). *Manual: A guide to the development and use of the Myers-Briggs Type Indicator*. Palo Alto, CA: Consulting Psychologists Press.

Naglieri, J. A. (1988). *Draw-a-Person: A quantitative scoring system*. San Antonio, TX: The Psychological Corporation.

Naglieri, J. A., & Pfeiffer, S. I. (1992). Performance of disruptive behavior disordered and normal samples on the Draw-a-Person: Screening procedure for emotional disturbance. *Psychological Assessment, 4*(2), 156-159.

Naglieri, J. A., McNeish, T. J., & Bardos, A. N. (1991). *Draw-a-Person: Screening procedure for emotional disturbance*. Austin, TX: Pro-Ed.

Naumberg, M. (1966). *Dynamically oriented art therapy: Its principles and practice, illustrated with three case studies*. New York: Grune & Stratton.

Newell, K., M., & Molenaar, P., C., M. (1998). *Applications of nonlinear dynamics to developmental process modeling.* Mahwah, NJ: Lawrence Erlbaum Associates.

Nijhoff, M. ed.(1893) Ouevres Completes de Christian Huyghens. *Societe Hollandaise des Sciences,* 5.

Offir, B., Bezalel, R., & Barth, I. (2007). Introverts, extroverts, and achievement in a distance learning environment. *American Journal of Distance Education, 21*(1), 3-19.

Oster, G. (1973). Auditory beats in the brain. *Scientific American, 229,* pp. 94-102.

Oster, G. D., & Crone, P. G. (2004). *Using drawing in assessment and therapy.* New York: Brunner-Routledge

Peratt, A. L. (2003). Characteristics for the Occurrence of a High-Current, Z-Pinch Aurora as Recorded in Antiquity. *IEEE Transactions on Plasma Science, 31* (6), 1192-1214.

Peretz, I. & Zatorre, R. J. (2005). Brain organization for music processing. *Annual Review of Psychology, 56*(1), 89-114.

Peterson, C. M. (2009). Relationship between Myers-Briggs Type Indicator Types and Projective Drawing Constructs. Walden University Thesis.

Peterson, L. W., & Hardin, M. E. (1997). *Children in distress: A guide for screening children's art.* New York: W. W. Norton.

Pfander, J., L., & Williams, B. A. (2006). The beat of a different drum: Using the arts in outreach to science/engineering students and faculty. *Issues in Science and Technology Librarianship, 3,* 1-9.

Picard, D., & Vinter, A. (1996). Relationships between procedural rigidity and interrepresentational change in children's drawing behavior. *Child Development, 78*(2), 522-541.

Power, S., & Lundsten, L. (1997). Studies that compare type theory and left-brain-right-brain theory. *Journal of Psychological Type, 43,* 22–28.

Protection of Human Subjects, 45 C.F.R. § 46 (2005).

Quenk, N. L., & Quenk, A. T. (1996). Counseling and psychotherapy. In A. L. Hammer (Ed.), *MBTI applications: A decade of research on the Myers-Briggs Type Indicator.* Mountain View, CA: CPP.

Ravaja, N., & Kallinen, K. (2004). Emotional effects of startling background music during reading news reports: The moderating influence f dispositional BIS and BAS sensitivities. *Scandinavian Journal of Psychology, 45,* 231-238.

Redmond, L. (1997). *When drummers were women: A spiritual history of rhythm.* New York, NY: Three Rivers Press.

Reynolds, C. R. (1978). A quick scoring guide to the interpretation of children's Kinetic Family Drawings (KFD). *Psychology in the School, 15*, 489-492.

Reynolds, C. R., & Hickman, J. A. (2004). *Draw-A-Person Intellectual Ability Test for Children, Adolescents, and Adults examiner's manual.* Austin, TX: Pro-Ed.

Rhyne, J. (1973). The gestalt art experience. Monterey, CA: Brooks/Coles.

Ross, C., Francis, L. J., & Craig, C. L. (2005). Dogmatism, religion, and psychological type. *Pastoral Psychology, 53*(5), 483-497.

Rosswurm, A., Pierson, B., & Woodward, L. (2007). The relationship between MBTI personality types and attachment styles of adults. *Psychology Journal, 4*(3), 109-127.

Roush, P. E., & Atwater, L. (1992). Using MBTI to understand self-perception accuracy. *Military Psychology, 4*(1), 17-34.

Sadakata, Ohgushi, & Desain, P. (2004). A cross-cultural comparison study of the production of simple rhythmic patterns. *Psychology of Music, 32*(4), 389-403.

Sak, U. (2004). A synthesis of research on psychological types of gifted adolescents. *The Journal of Secondary Gifted Education, 15*(2), 70-79.

Salter, D. W., & Junco, R. (2007). Measuring small-group environments. A validity study of scores from the Salter Environmental Type Assessment and the Group Environment Scale. *Educational and Psychological Measurement, 67*, 475-486.

Scherer, K. R. (2004). Which emotions can be induced by music? What are the underlying Mechanisms? And how can we measure them? *Journal of New Music Research, 33*, 239-251

Schrodinger, E. (1982) *Collected papers on wave mechanics* (3rd ed.) New York: Chelsea Publishing Company.

Schultz, L. H., & Selman, R. L. (1989). Bridging the gap between interpersonal thought and action in early adolescence: The role of psychodynamic processes. *Psychopathology, 1*(2), 133-152.

Schwartz, K. (2004). Music preferences, personality, style, and developmental issues of adolescents. *The Journal of Youth Ministry, 3*, 47-64.

Shank, M., & Langmeyer, L. (1994). Does personality influence brand image? *Journal of Psychology, 128*(2), 157-164.

Shin'ya, U., Hiroshi, M., Hideo, U., & Gyu, P., G. (2005). Study on entrainment between walking rhythm of many pedestrians and oscillation of the bridge. Dynamics & Design Conference CDROM2005, 521.

Shipman, F., Airhart, R., Hsieh, H., Maloor, P., Moore, J. M., & Shah, D. (2001). Visual and spatial communication and task organization using visual knowledge builder. *Proceedings of the 2001 International ACM SIGGROUP Conference on Supporting Group Work* (pp. 260-269). New York: ACM.

Shulman K. J., Gold, D., Cohen, C., & Zucchero, C. (1993) Clock-drawing test drawing and dementia in the community: A longitudinal study. *International Journal of Geriatric Psychology, 8*, 487-496.

Slachmuijlder, L. (2005). The rhythm of reconciliation: A reflection on drumming as a contribution to reconciliation process in Burundi and South Africa a working paper recasting reconciliation through culture and the arts. Coexistence International Waltham, MA: Brandeis University. Retrieved January 8, 2008, from http://www.brandeis.edu/programs/Slifka/vrc/ papers/lena/Slachmuijlder.pdf.

Slifer, D., Nakai, D. & Mirabal, R. W. (2007). *Kokopelli: The Magic, Mirth, and Mischief of an Ancient Symbol.* Layton, Utah: Gibbs Smith.

Smith, K. C., & Cuddy, L. L. (1989). Effects of metric and harmonic rhythm on the detection of pitch alteration in melodic sequences. *Journal of Experimental Psychology, 15*, 457-471.

Spensley, F., & Taylor, J. (1999). The development of cognitive flexibility: Evidence from children's drawings. *Human Development, 42*, 300-324

Sperry, R. W. (1975) Left-brain, right-brain. *Saturday Review.* Aug. 9, pp. 30-33

Spoor, P. S. & Swift, G., W. (2000). The Huygens entrainment phenomenon and thermoacoutistic engines. *Acoustical Society of America, 108*(2), 588 -599.

Stecker, R. (2001). Expressiveness and expression in music and poetry. *The Journal of Aesthetics and Art Criticism, 59*, 85-96.

Stevens, C. (2003). *The art and heart of drum circles.* Milwaukee, WI: Hal Leonard.

Stevens, C. (2004). Cross-cultural studies of musical pitch and time. *Acoustic Science & Technology, 25*(6), 433-438.

Stuart, J. J., Western, D., Lohr, N. E., & Benjamin, J. (1990). Object relations in borderlines, depressives, and normals: An examination of human responses on the Rorschach. *Journal of Personality Assessment, 55*(1/2), 296-318.

Talbot, D. (2009). Symbols of an Alien Sky, Part Three. Video: retrieved from http://www.thunderbolts.info

Tharinger, D. J., & Stark, K. D. (1990). A qualitative versus quantitative approach to evaluating the Draw-A-Person and Kinetic Family Drawing: A study of mood- and anxiety-disorder children. *Psychological Assessment: A Journal of Consulting and Clinical Psychology, 2*(4), 365-375.

.

Varvel, T., Adams, S., Pridie, S., & Ruiz Ulloa, B. (2004). Team effectiveness and individual Myers-Briggs personality dimensions. *Journal of Management in Engineering, 20*(4), 141-146.

Vastfjall, D., Larson, P., & Kleiner, M. (2002). Emotion and auditory virtual environments: Affect-based judgments of music reproduced with virtual reverberation times. *CyberPsychology & Behavior, 5*(1), 19-32.

Wadeson, H. (1980). *Art psychotherapy.* New York: John Wiley & Sons.

Watson Y. I., Arfken, C. L., & Birge, S. J. (1993). Clock completion: An objective screening test for dementia. *Journal of American Geriatric Society, 41*, 1235-1240.

Webster G. D., & Weir C. G. (2005). Emotional responses to music: Interactive effects of mode, texture, and tempo. *Motivation and Emotion, 29*(1), 19-39.

Westen, D. (1992). Social cognition and object relations. *Psychological Bulletin, 109*, 429-455.

Westen, D., Lohr, N., Silk, K., Gould, L., & Kerber, K. (1990) Object relations and social cognition in borderlines, major depressives, and normals: A TAT analysis. *Psychological Assessment: A Journal of Consulting and Clinical Psychology, 2*, 355-364.

Wheeler, P. R., Hunton, J. E., & Bryant, S. M. (2004). Accounting information systems research opportunities using personality type theory an the Myers-Briggs Type Indicator. *Journal of Information Systems, 18*(1), 1-19.

Whiteley, S. (1997). Sexing the groove: Popular music and gender. New York: Rutledge.

Williams, T. O., Fall, A., Eaves, R. C., & Woods-Groves, S. (2006). The reliability of scores for the Draw-A-Person Intellectual Ability Test for Children, Adolescents, and Adults. *Journal of Psychoeducational Assessment, 24*(2), 137-146.

Winkelman, M. (2003). Complementary therapy for addiction: Druming out drugs. *American Journal of Public Health, 93*, 647-651.

Woody, R. H. (2002). Emotion, imagery, and metaphor in the acquisition of musical performance skill. *Music Education Research, 4*, 213-224.

Wu, S., Lin C. S. and Lin T. (2006). Exploring knowledge sharing in virtual teams: A social exchange theory perspective. *Proceedings of the 39th Hawaii International Conference on System Sciences.* 1-10.

Yalen, L. & Cohen, C. (2007) Complementary approaches to coexistence work: Focus on coexistence and the arts. Coexistence International Waltham, MA: Brandeis University. Retrieved January 8, 2008 from: http://www.coexistence.net.

Yoshino, I., & Abe, J. (2004). Cognitive modeling of key interpretation in melody perception.

Japanese Psychological Research, 46, 283-297.

Zhi, Z., Thomas, G. V., & Robinson, E. J. (1997). Constraints on representational change: Drawing a man with two heads. *British Journal of Developmental Psychology, 15*, 275-290.

Index

About the Author:

C. M. Peterson

M.S. Psychology, B.S. Physics, PMP

cynthia@cp.gccoxmail.com